A Kodansha Comics Trade Paperback Original.

Hitorijime My Hero volume 3 copyright © 2014 Memeco Arii
English translation copyright © 2019 Memeco Arii

Published in the United States by Kodansha Comics,
an imprint of Kodansha USA Publishing, LLC, New York.

Publication rights for this English edition arranged through Kodansha
Ltd., Tokyo.

First published in Japan in 2014 by Ichijinsha Inc., Tokyo.

ISBN 978-1-63236-773-0

Printed in the United States of America.

www.kodanshacomics.com

9 8 7 6 5 4 3

Translation: Anne Lee
Lettering: Michael Martin
Editing: Lauren Scanlan, Haruko Hashimoto
Kodansha Comics Edition Cover Design: Phil Balsman

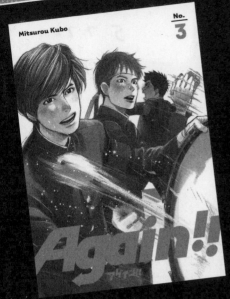

No. **3**

Mitsurou Kubo

Again!!
アゲイン!!

Kinichiro Imamura isn't a bad guy, really, but on the first day of high school his narrow eyes and bleached blonde hair made him look so shifty that his classmates assumed the worst. Three years later, without any friends or fond memories, he isn't exactly feeling bittersweet about graduation. But after an accidental fall down a flight of stairs, Kinichiro wakes up three years in the past... on the first day of high school. School's starting again—but it's gonna be different this time around!

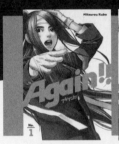

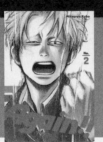

Vol. 1-3 now available in PRINT and DIGITAL!
Vol. 4 coming August 2018!
Find out **MORE** by visiting:
kodanshacomics.com/MitsurouKubo

ABOUT **MITSUROU KUBO**

Mitsurou Kubo is a manga artist born in Nagasaki prefecture. Her series *3.3.7 Byoshi!!* (2001-2003), *Tokkyu!!* (2004-2008), and *Again!!* (2011-2014) were published in *Weekly Shonen Magazine*, and *Moteki* (2008-2010) was published in the seinen comics magazine *Evening*. After the publication of *Again!!* concluded, she met Sayo Yamamoto, director of the global smash-hit anime *Yuri!!! on ICE*. Working with Yamamoto, Kubo contributed the original concept, original character designs, and initial script for *Yuri!!! on ICE*. *Again!!* is her first manga to be published in English.

KC KODANSHA COMICS

KodanshaCOMICS

KC

KODANSHA
COMICS

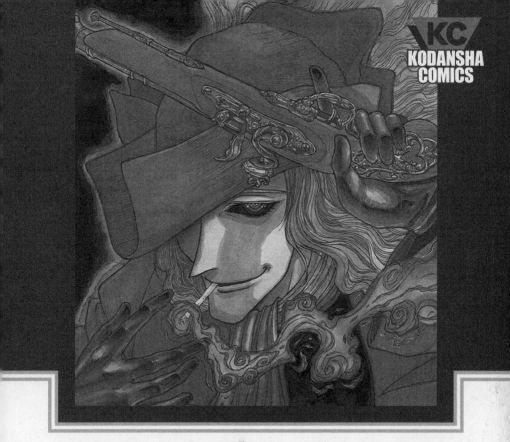

The Black Museum The Ghost and the Lady

By Kazuhiro Fujita

Deep in Scotland Yard in London sits an evidence room dedicated to the greatest mysteries of British history. In this "Black Museum" sits a misshapen hunk of lead—two bullets fused together—the key to a wartime encounter between Florence Nightingale, the mother of modern nursing, and a supernatural Man in Grey. This story is unknown to most scholars of history, but a special guest of the museum will tell the tale of The Ghost and the Lady...

Praise for Kazuhiro Fujita's *Ushio and Tora*

"A charming revival that combines a classic look with modern depth and pacing... **Essential viewing both for curmudgeons and new fans alike.**" — Anime News Network

"**GREAT!** The first episode of Ushio and Tora captures the essence of '90s anime." — IGN

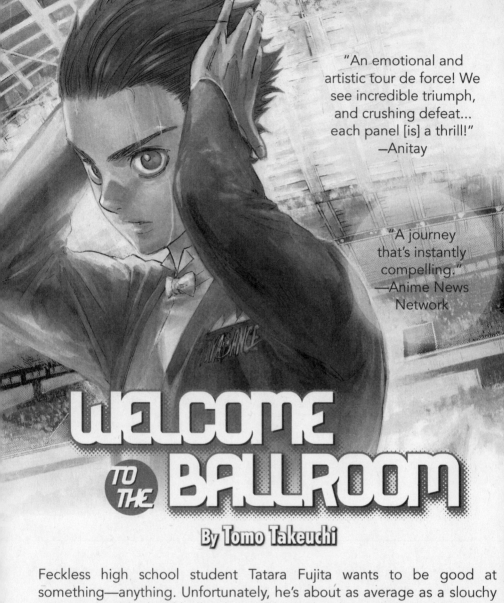

"An emotional and artistic tour de force! We see incredible triumph, and crushing defeat... each panel [is] a thrill!"
—Anitay

"A journey that's instantly compelling."
—Anime News Network

WELCOME TO THE BALLROOM

By Tomo Takeuchi

Feckless high school student Tatara Fujita wants to be good at something—anything. Unfortunately, he's about as average as a slouchy teen can be. The local bullies know this, and make it a habit to hit him up for cash, but all that changes when the debonair Kaname Sengoku sends them packing. Sengoku's not the neighborhood watch, though. He's a professional ballroom dancer. And once Tatara Fujita gets pulled into the world of ballroom, his life will never be the same.

KC KODANSHA COMICS

Having lost his wife, high school teacher Kōhei Inuzuka is doing his best to raise his young daughter Tsumugi as a single father. He's pretty bad at cooking and doesn't have a huge appetite to begin with, but chance brings his little family together with one of his students, the lonely Kotori. The three of them are anything but comfortable in the kitchen, but the healing power of home cooking might just work on their grieving hearts.

"This season's number-one feel-good anime!" —Anime News Network

"A beautifully-drawn story about comfort food and family and grief. Recommended." —Otaku USA Magazine

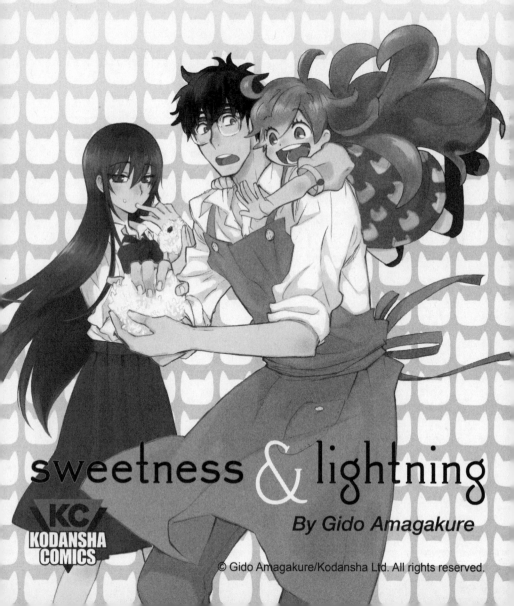

sweetness & lightning

By Gido Amagakure

KC
KODANSHA
COMICS

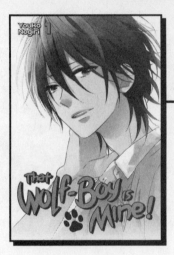
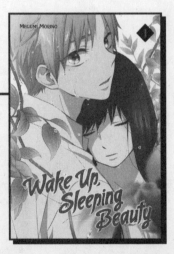

WAITING FOR SPRING

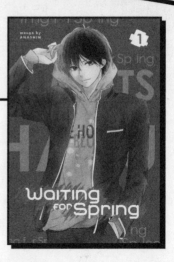

A sweet romantic story of a soft-spoken high school freshman and her quest to make friends. For fans of earnest, fun, and dramatic shojo like *Kimi ni Todoke* and *Say I Love You.*

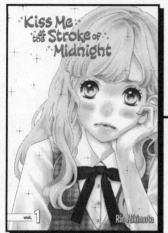

KISS ME AT THE STROKE OF MIDNIGHT

An all-new Cinderella comedy perfect for fans of *My Little Monster* and *Say I Love You!*

LOVE AND LIES

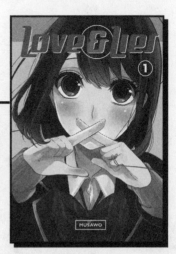

Love is forbidden. When you turn 16, the government will assign you your marriage partner. This dystopian manga about teen love and defiance is a sexy, funny, and dramatic new hit! Anime now streaming on Anime Strike!

A new series from Yoshitoki Oima, creator of The New York Times bestselling manga and Eisner Award nominee *A Silent Voice*!

An intimate, emotional drama and an epic story spanning time and space...

TO YOUR ETERNITY

An orb was cast unto the earth. After metamorphosing into a wolf, It joins a boy on his bleak journey to find his tribe. Ever learning, It transcends death, even when those around It cannot...

NO.6

A PERFECT LIFE IN A PERFECT CITY

For Shion, an elite student in the technologically sophisticated city No. 6, life is carefully choreographed. One fateful day, he takes a misstep, sheltering a fugitive his age from a typhoon. Helping this boy throws Shion's life down a path to discovering the appalling secrets behind the "perfection" of No. 6.

gateau, page 175

gateau is the manga magazine *Hitorijime My Hero* is serialized in in Japan before its released as the *tankobon* book version you're reading now!

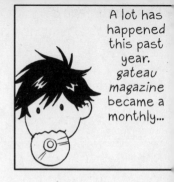

Boyfriend, page 175

Before *Hitorijime My Hero,* Memeco Arii released a single volume prequel manga about Kensuke Ohshiba and Asaya Hasekura titled *Hitorijime My Boyfriend.*

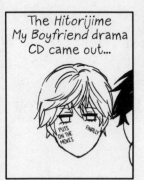

Oropon, page 177

Oropon is a portmanteau of *"oroshi"* and *"ponzu."* It is a sauce made with *oroshi daikon* (grated white radish) and a savory citrus sauce. It is often served as a dipping sauce for meat.

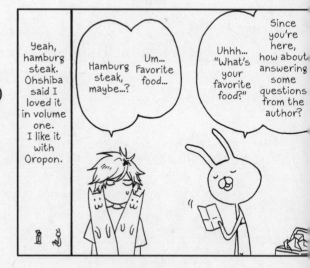

Ehomaki, page 85
An *ehomaki* is a sushi roll eaten during *Setsubun* for good luck. It's considered lucky to roll ingredients representing the *Shichifukujin,* or Seven Gods of Good Fortune, into the *ehomaki* filling.

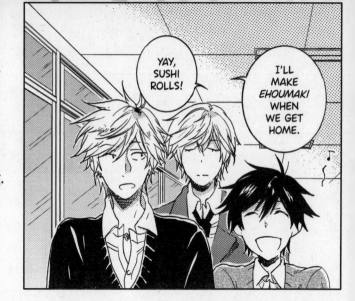

Oni, page 89
In the *mamemaki* bean scattering ritual held on *Setsubun*, a family member (usually a parent) wears a mask and pretends to be a demon, or *oni*, while other members of the family (usually the children) throw beans at them while yelling *"Oni wa soto!"* (Demons out!).

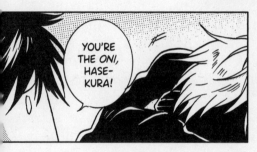

Curtain, page 117
The curtain Masahiro is referring to is called a *noren*, a short curtain hung in the doorway of stores when they are open for business. Many stores, like Shoufuku Ramen, have their name or logo printed on the curtain.

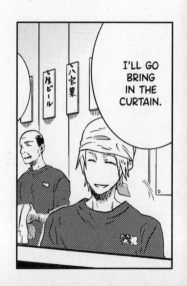

Shaggy eyebrows, page 61

Kensuke is referring to the fact that the *"shige"* of Shigeo sounds like the Japanese verb for growing thickly, or *shigeru.* It's both a reference to Shigeo's particularly prominent eyebrows and the Japanese actor Shigeo Takamatsu, who also has very distinctive eyebrows.

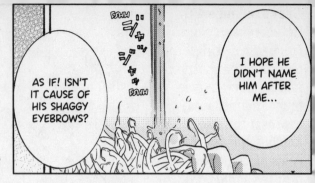

AS IF! ISN'T IT CAUSE OF HIS SHAGGY EYEBROWS?

I HOPE HE DIDN'T NAME HIM AFTER ME...

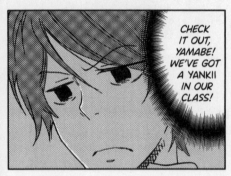

CHECK IT OUT, YAMABE! WE'VE GOT A YANKII IN OUR CLASS!

Yankii, page 81

Yankii is a borrowed term from the English, "yankee," referring to the original inspiration from the post-WWII American GI culture of bad boys and rock n' roll. Most often translated as *"juvenile delinquent,"* yankii reject social norms, manners, and expectations with flair. Stereotypically, yankii are known for their rebellious attitude—all of which comes through their affected language, big and often bleached-blond hairstyles, and flashy clothing. Yankii groups, like any gang, still maintain their own codes of honor, along with hierarchies.

Setsubun, page 85

Setsubun is a Japanese holiday occurring on February 3rd, the day before spring. To drive away evil spirits and bring good luck into the household, families scatter beans in a ritual called *mamemaki,* shouting *"Oni wa soto! Fuku wa uchi!"* (Demons out! Good luck in!).

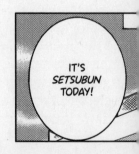

IT'S SETSUBUN TODAY!

Gravure, page 49

In Japan, the usage of "gravure" comes from the English term "rotogravure," a printing process often used for printing images in magazines. Now, "gravure" in Japan most commonly refers to "gravure models/idols" and "gravure magazines" which feature suggestive photos of young women. Though the gravure industry is aimed at older audiences, it is mainly non-explicit in content. It centers on young women posing in swim suits, building an appealing public persona, and selling photobooks and merchandise. Gravure idols are just like any other celebrity in the entertainment industry, and the label itself is quite fluid.

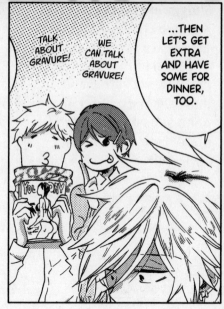

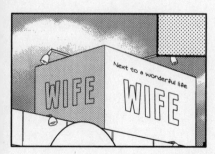

Wife, page 50

A pun on the Japanese supermarket chain called Life.

Student council chairman, page 54

In Japan, high schools have a student council consisting of members elected by the student body that oversee club activities, help organize events, make sure other students follow school rules, and more. Chairman is the chairman of the student council, which is where he got his nickname. Since he's been re-elected, it could be quite a while until we learn his real name!

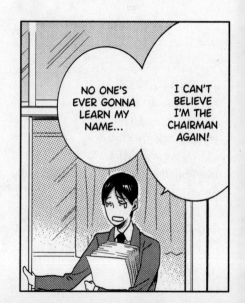

Katsudon, page 11

Katsudon is a popular Japanese meal consisting of a bowl of rice topped with egg and a breaded and fried pork cutlet. It often appears as a meal offered during interrogation scenes.

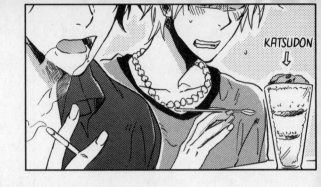

MonHun, page 13

MonHun is short for *Monster Hunter*, a popular third-person action video game series by Capcom. In it, players assume the role of a hunter with up to three friends and track and battle giant fantastical monsters such as dragons.

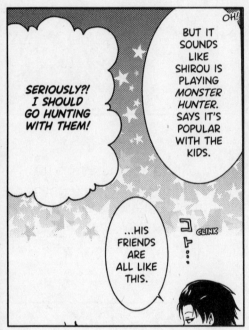

Imonikai, page 44

An *imonikai* is an outdoor party where guests stew various types of vegetables and potatoes.

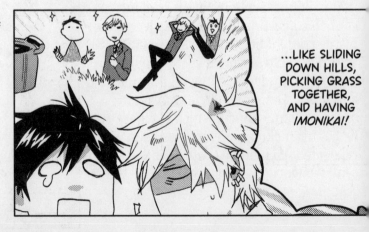

Translation Notes

Kamikaze hitman, page 5
Kousuke is actually asked if he was a *teppoudama*, which literally translates to "a bullet." It refers to a hitman who is sent on an assignment from which he is not expected to return alive, like a bullet that enters a body.

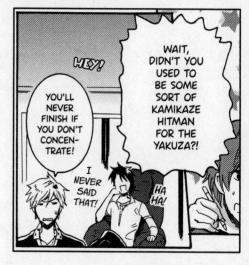

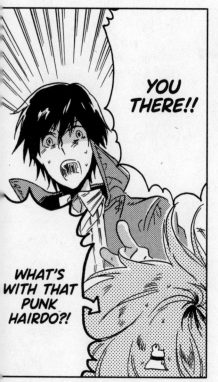

Punk hairdo, page 10
Masahiro's blond, bleached hair is often associated with delinquents, punks, and members of counterculture scenes in Japan. That isn't always the case, of course.

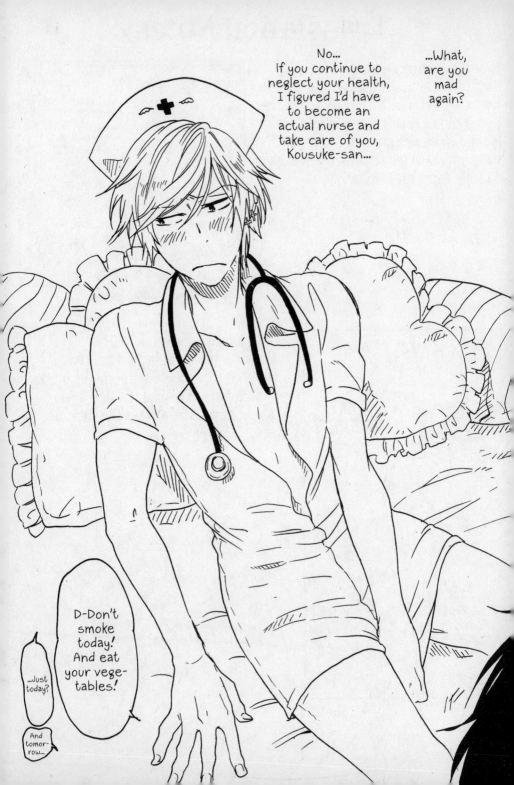

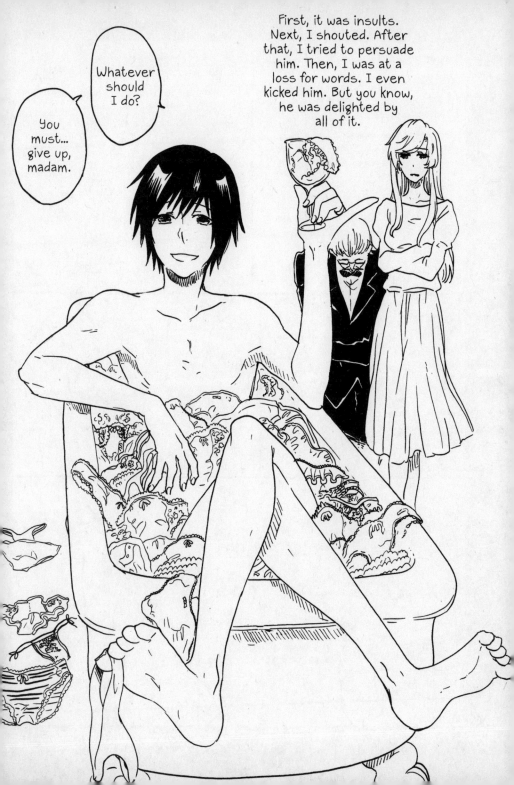

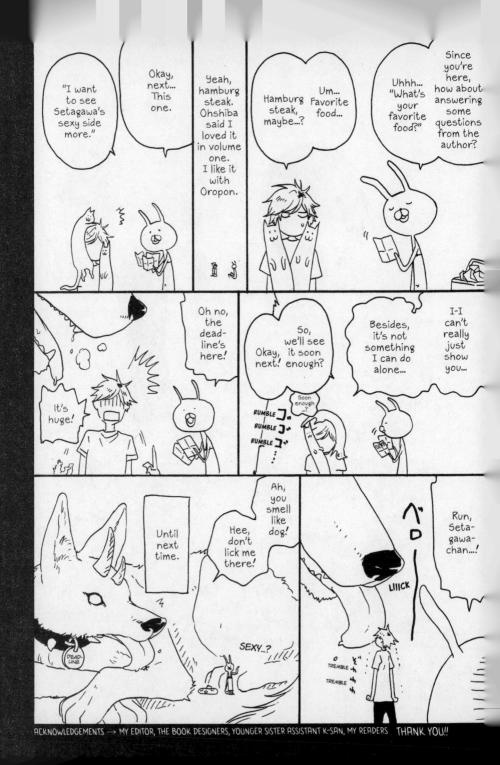

ACKNOWLEDGEMENTS → MY EDITOR, THE BOOK DESIGNERS, YOUNGER SISTER ASSISTANT K-SAN, MY READERS THANK YOU!!

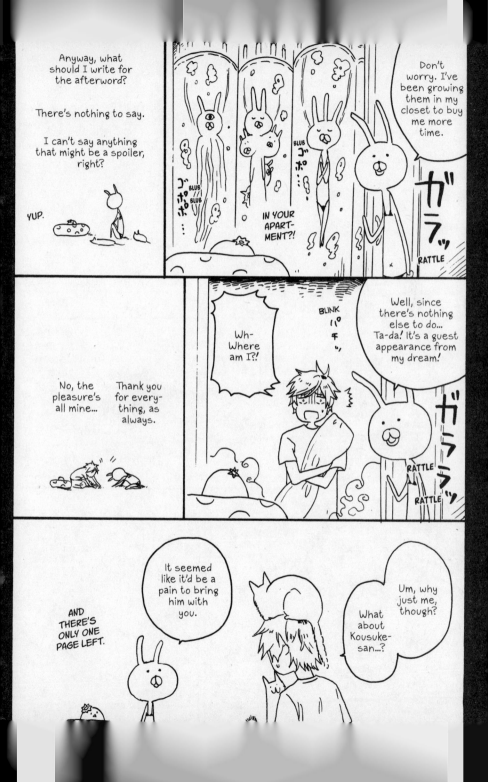

Melting Afterword

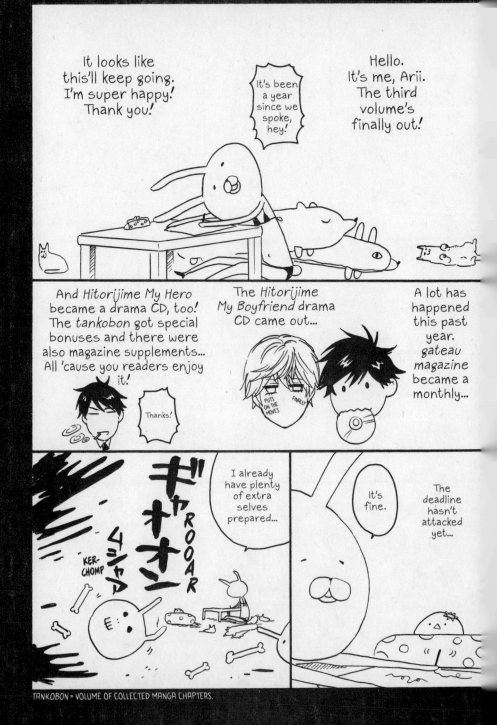

It looks like this'll keep going. I'm super happy! Thank you!

It's been a year since we spoke, hey!

Hello. It's me, Arii. The third volume's finally out!

And *Hitorijime My Hero* became a drama CD, too! The *tankobon* got special bonuses and there were also magazine supplements... All 'cause you readers enjoy it!

Thanks!

The *Hitorijime My Boyfriend* drama CD came out...

PUTS ON THE MOVES

FINALLY

A lot has happened this past year. *gateau magazine* became a monthly...

GYANROOAR

KER-CHOMP

I already have plenty of extra selves prepared...

It's fine.

The deadline hasn't attacked yet...

TANKOBON = VOLUME OF COLLECTED MANGA CHAPTERS.

Hitorijime My Hero

FIRST
RUN ★

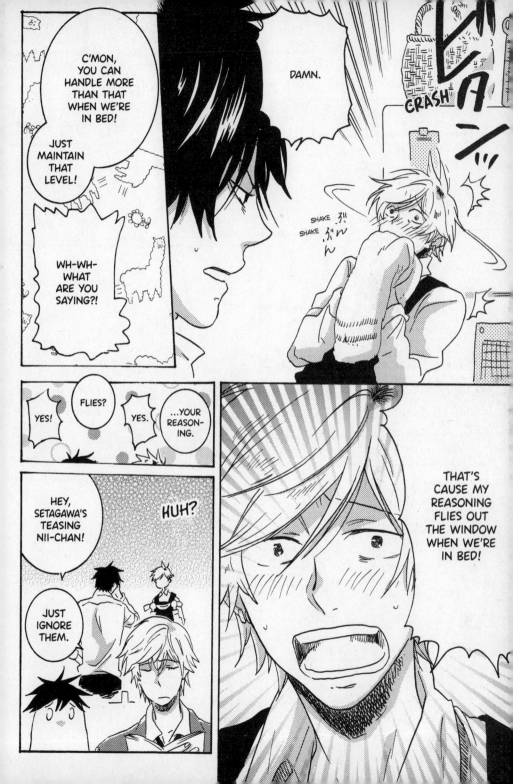

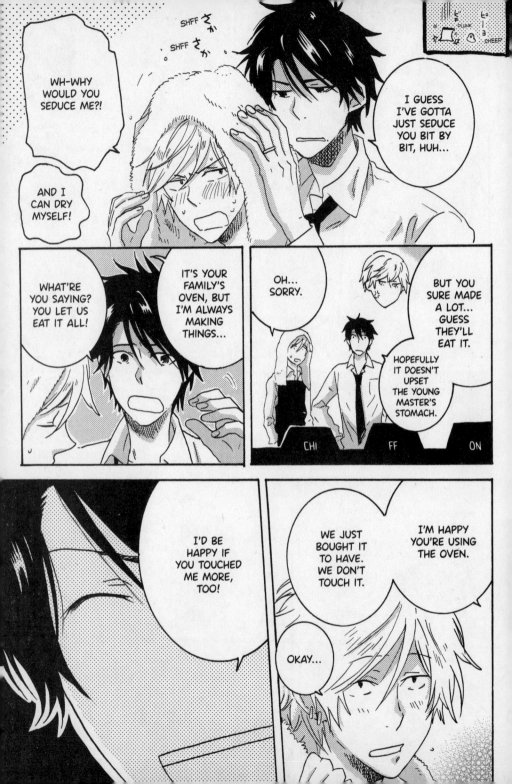

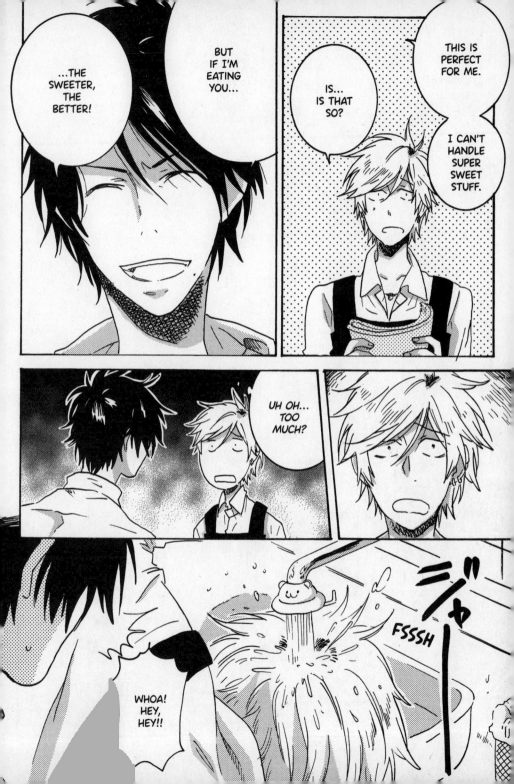

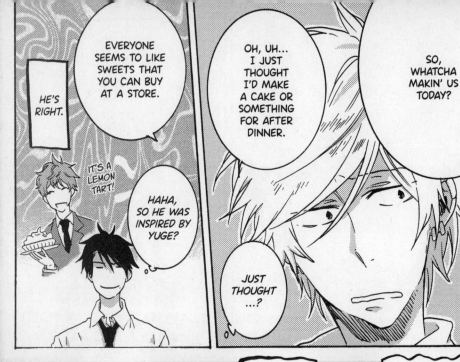

EVERYONE SEEMS TO LIKE SWEETS THAT YOU CAN BUY AT A STORE.

HE'S RIGHT.

IT'S A LEMON TART!

HAHA, SO HE WAS INSPIRED BY YUGE?

OH, UH... I JUST THOUGHT I'D MAKE A CAKE OR SOMETHING FOR AFTER DINNER.

JUST THOUGHT ...?

SO, WHATCHA MAKIN' US TODAY?

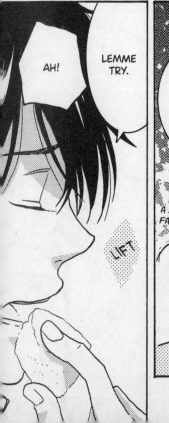

AH!

LEMME TRY.

LIFT

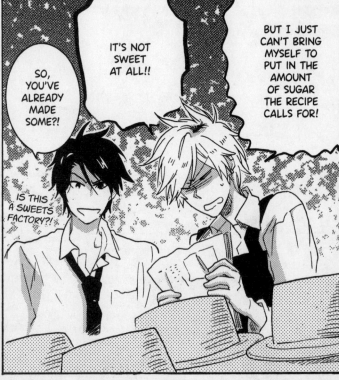

SO, YOU'VE ALREADY MADE SOME?!

IS THIS A SWEETS FACTORY?!

IT'S NOT SWEET AT ALL!!

BUT I JUST CAN'T BRING MYSELF TO PUT IN THE AMOUNT OF SUGAR THE RECIPE CALLS FOR!

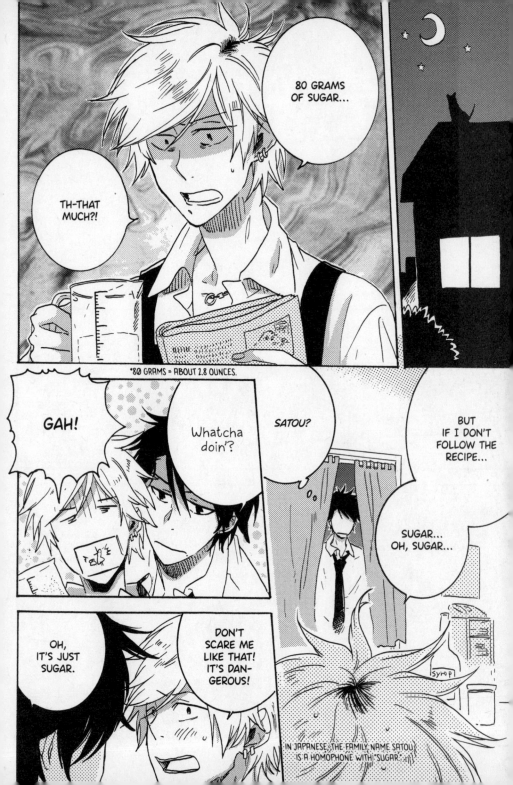

80 GRAMS OF SUGAR...

TH-THAT MUCH?!

*80 GRAMS = ABOUT 2.8 OUNCES.

GAH!

Whatcha doin'?

SATOU?

BUT IF I DON'T FOLLOW THE RECIPE...

SUGAR... OH, SUGAR...

OH, IT'S JUST SUGAR.

DON'T SCARE ME LIKE THAT! IT'S DANGEROUS!

IN JAPANESE, THE FAMILY NAME SATOU IS A HOMOPHONE WITH "SUGAR".

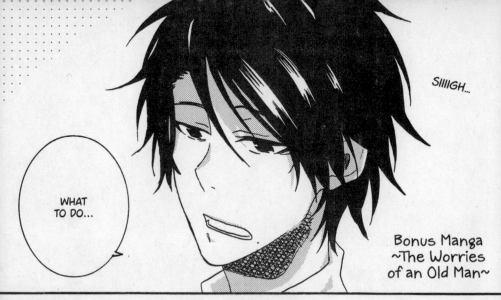

SIIIIGH...

WHAT TO DO...

Bonus Manga
~The Worries
of an Old Man~

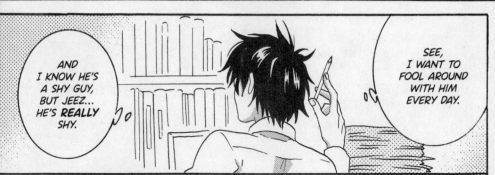

AND I KNOW HE'S A SHY GUY, BUT JEEZ... HE'S **REALLY** SHY.

SEE, I WANT TO FOOL AROUND WITH HIM EVERY DAY.

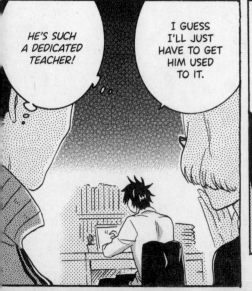

HE'S SUCH A DEDICATED TEACHER!

I GUESS I'LL JUST HAVE TO GET HIM USED TO IT.

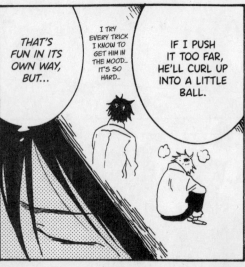

THAT'S FUN IN ITS OWN WAY, BUT...

I TRY EVERY TRICK I KNOW TO GET HIM IN THE MOOD... IT'S SO HARD...

IF I PUSH IT TOO FAR, HE'LL CURL UP INTO A LITTLE BALL.

Hitorijime My Hero

Sometimes chews them.

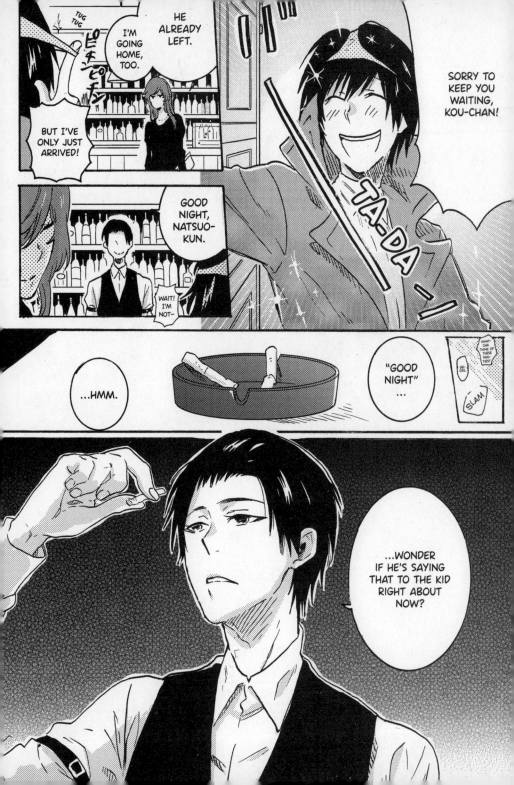

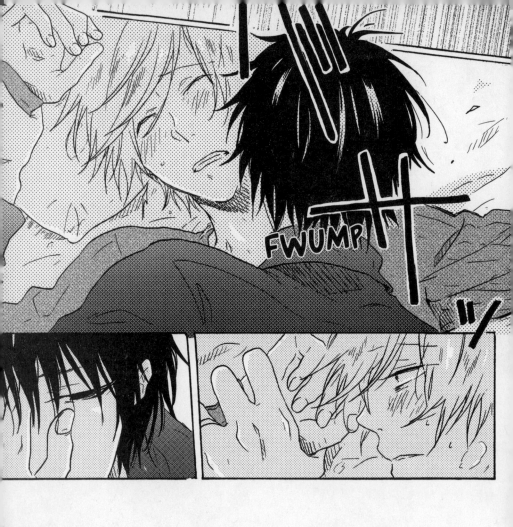

JUST FOR NOW...

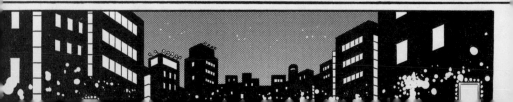

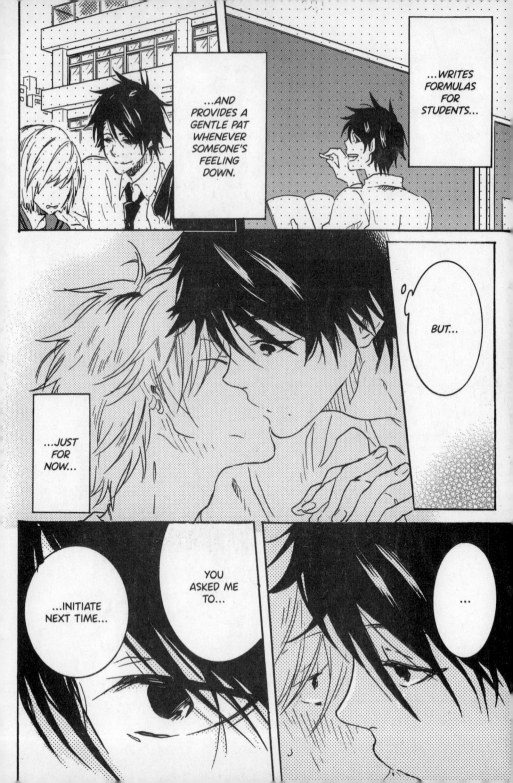

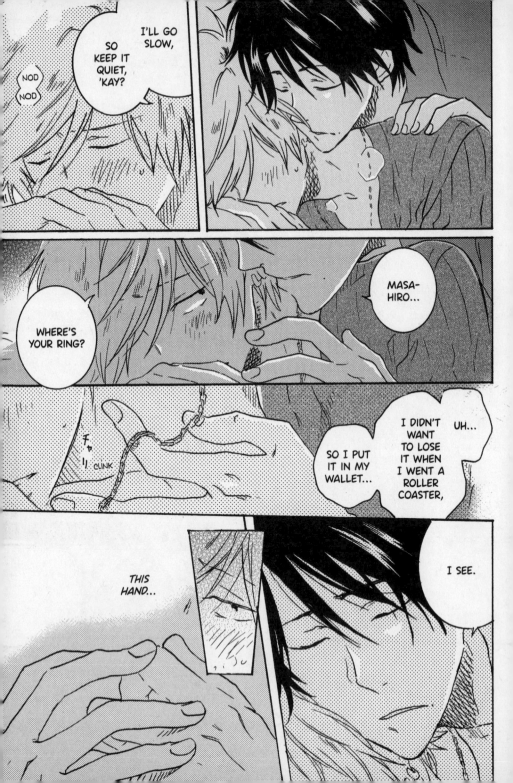

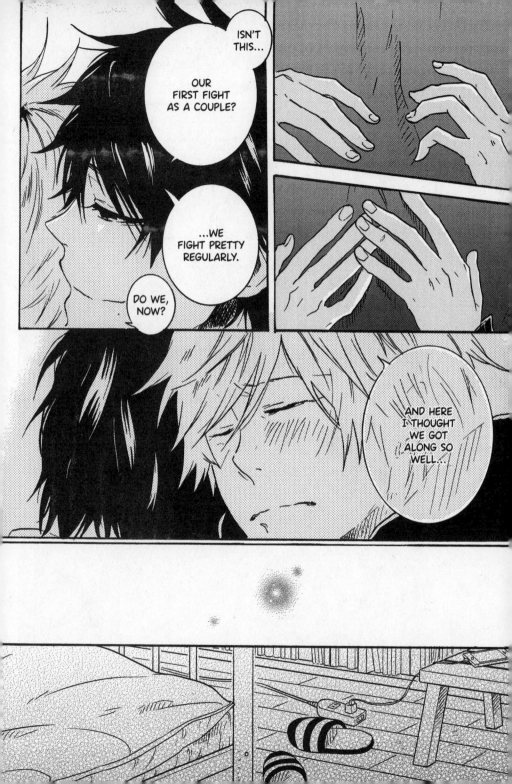

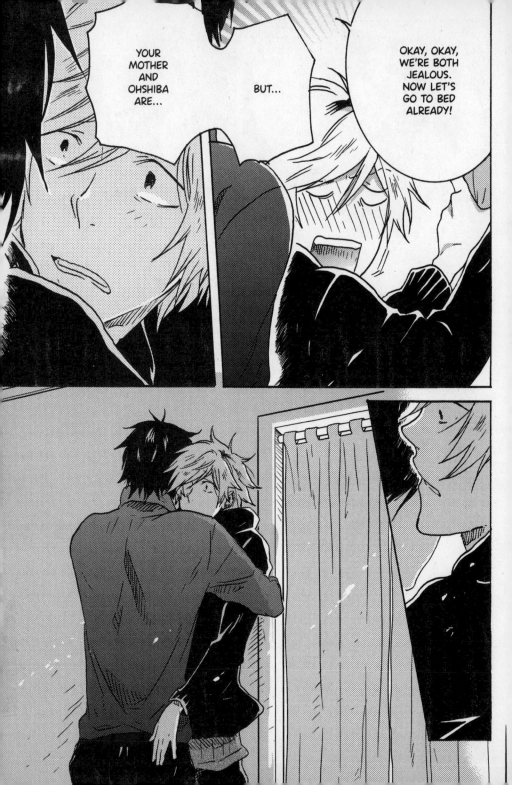

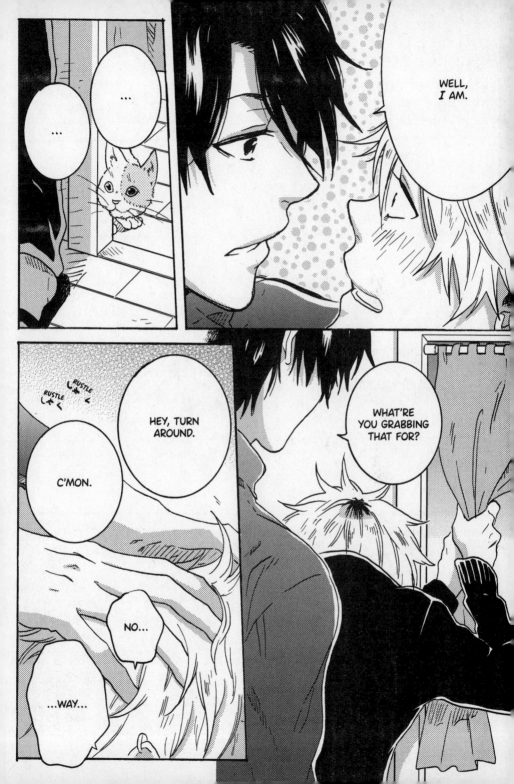

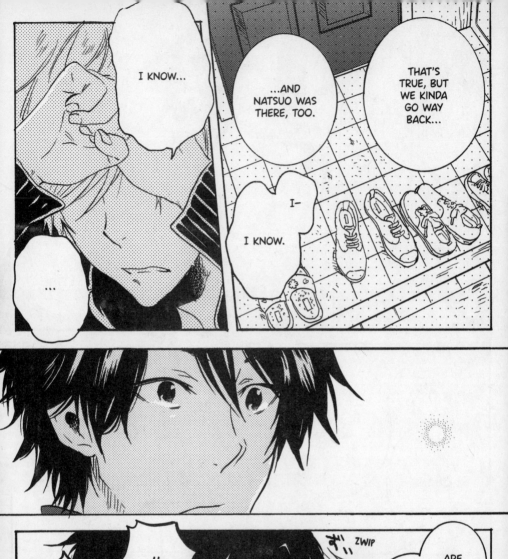

I KNOW...

...AND NATSUO WAS THERE, TOO.

THAT'S TRUE, BUT WE KINDA GO WAY BACK...

I-

I KNOW.

...

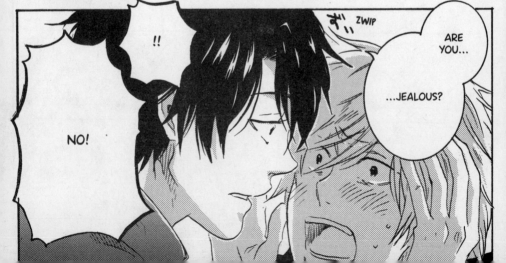

ZWIP

!!

NO!

ARE YOU...

...JEALOUS?

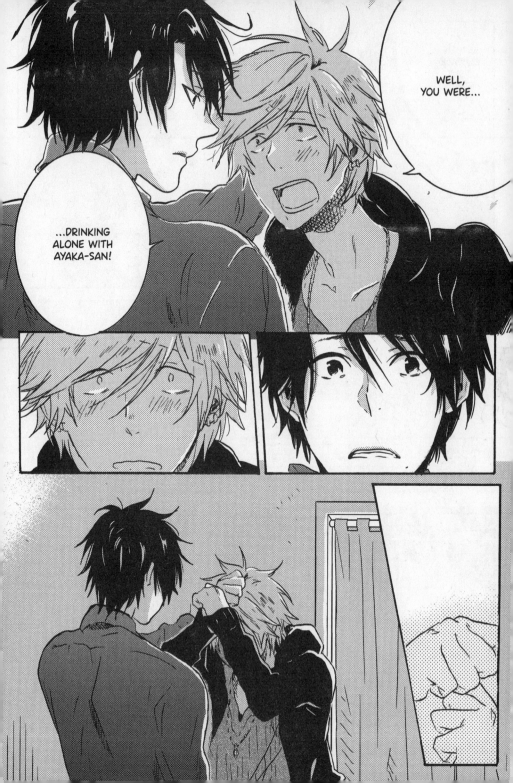

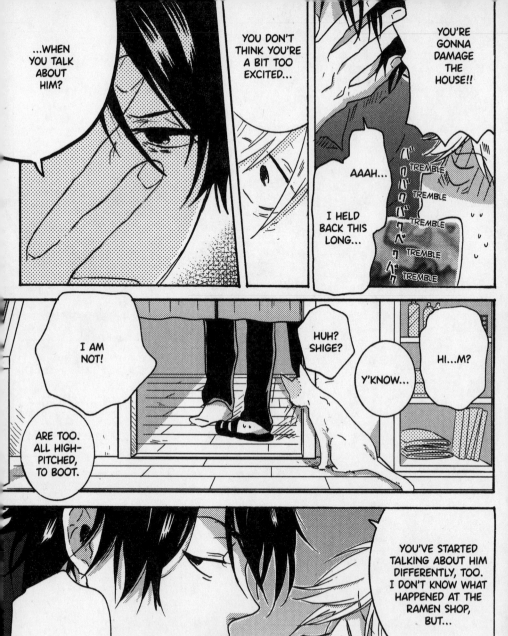

...WHEN YOU TALK ABOUT HIM?

YOU DON'T THINK YOU'RE A BIT TOO EXCITED...

YOU'RE GONNA DAMAGE THE HOUSE!!

AAAH...

I HELD BACK THIS LONG...

TREMBLE

TREMBLE

TREMBLE

TREMBLE

TREMBLE

I AM NOT!

ARE TOO. ALL HIGH-PITCHED, TO BOOT.

HUH? SHIGE?

Y'KNOW...

HI...M?

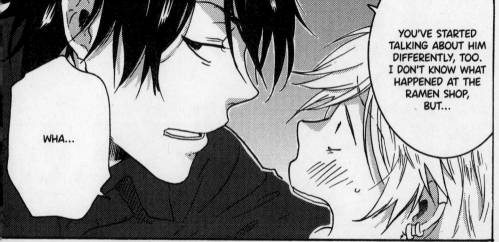

WHA...

YOU'VE STARTED TALKING ABOUT HIM DIFFERENTLY, TOO. I DON'T KNOW WHAT HAPPENED AT THE RAMEN SHOP, BUT...

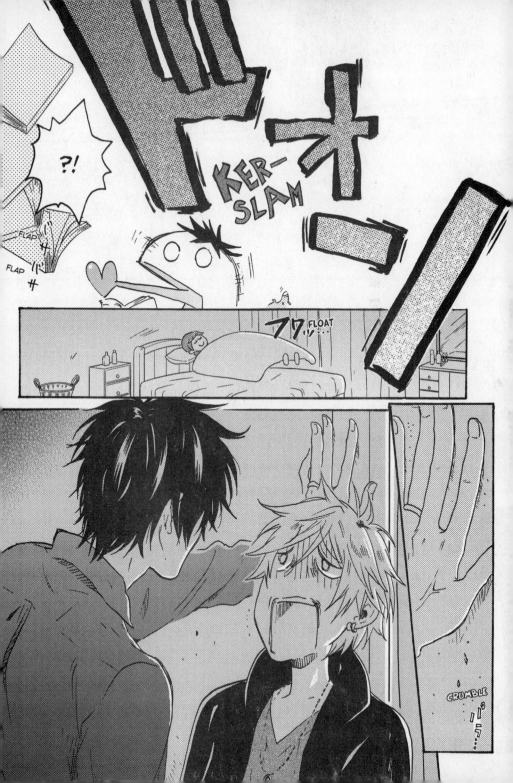

...HE TOTALLY SHRIEKED WHEN A ZOMBIE JUMPED OUT...

EVEN THOUGH HE SAID THAT KIND OF THING DIDN'T INTEREST HIM...

I WISH YOU COULD'VE SEEN IT, KOUSUKE-SAN!

AND ON TOP OF THAT, HE CLUNG ONTO ME AND OHSHIBA!

HAH!

SHINE

WELL, ONCE MOM FALLS ASLEEP SHE DOESN'T WAKE UP, SO IT SHOULD BE OKAY IF THEY KEEP IT QUIET!

WHAT SHOULD I DO IF THEY START FOOLIN' AROUND?

I WONDER IF ONII-CHAN AND SETAGAWA WERE ABLE TO TALK...

HEHE

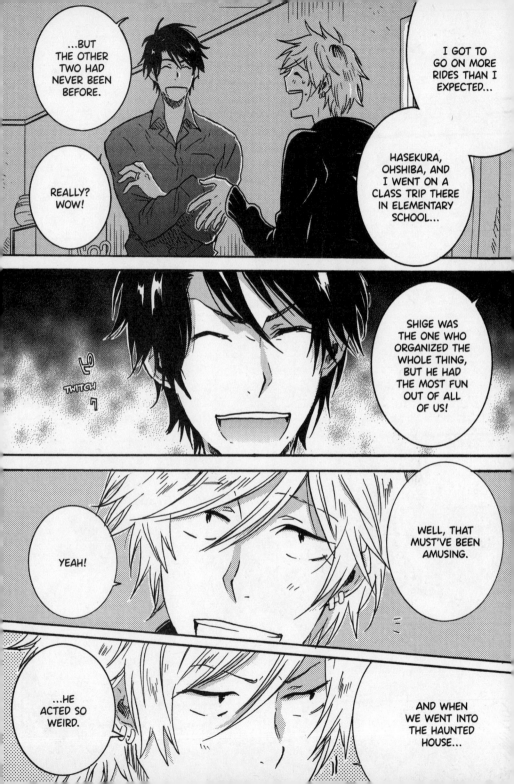

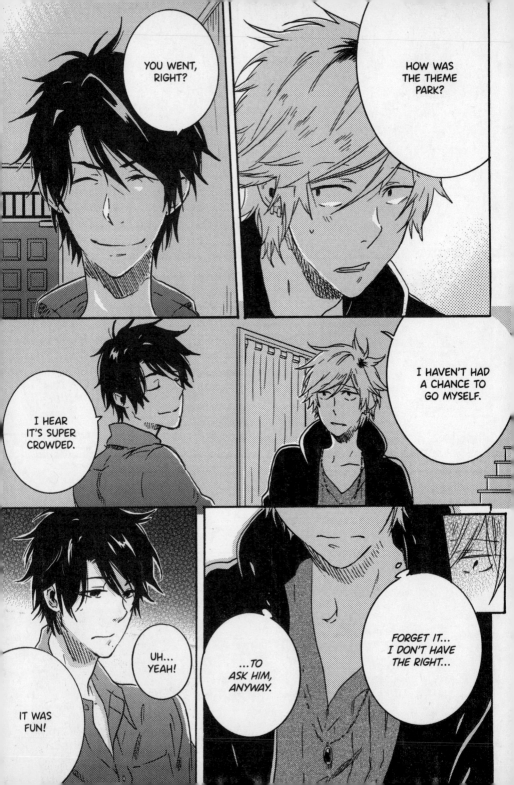

WERE YOU WAITING FOR ME, BY ANY CHANCE?

THUMP

THUMP

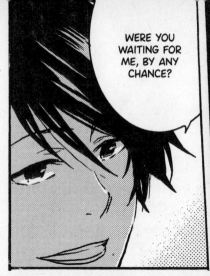

SLAM

IF YOU SENT A MESSAGE, I WOULD'VE COME BACK RIGHT AWAY.

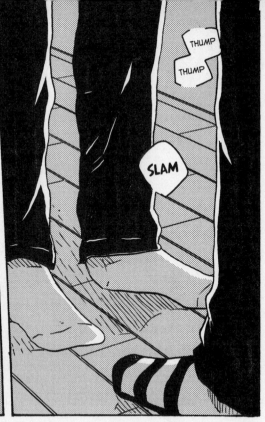

WOW, YOU WERE OUT HAVIN' FUN PRETTY LATE!

THAT RIGHT?!

I WASN'T WAITING FOR YOU!

N-NO, I JUST GOT BACK MYSELF!

I CAN'T SAY I WAS WAITING FOR HIM TO MESSAGE ME...

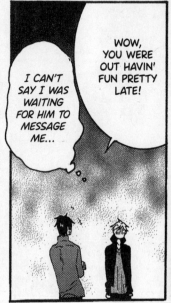

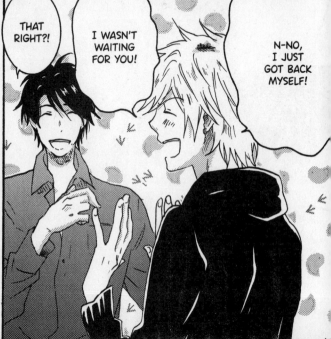

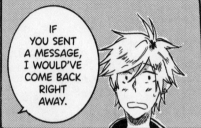

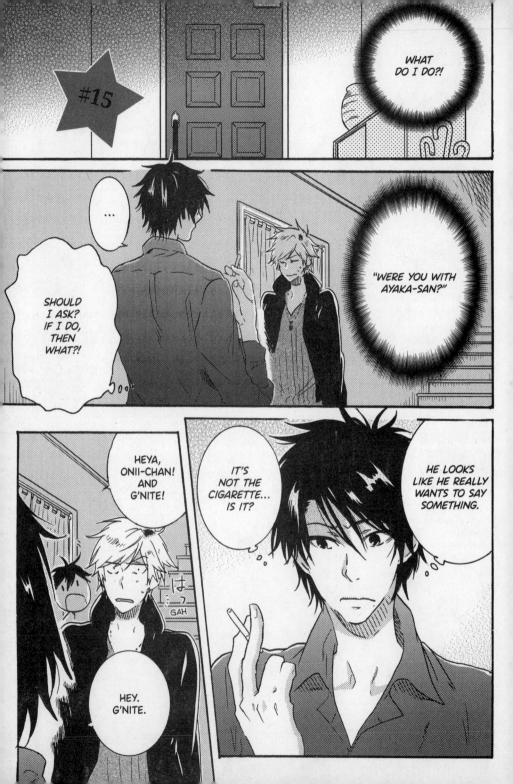

Hitorijime My Hero

Everyone's Favorite

Boing Boing
        Pow Pow Pow Land

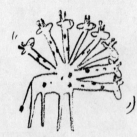

The main attraction
is the talk of the town.
Eight-Headed Giraffe
According to park-goer
S-kun, "it's massive and
wobbles all around.
It's pretty scary."

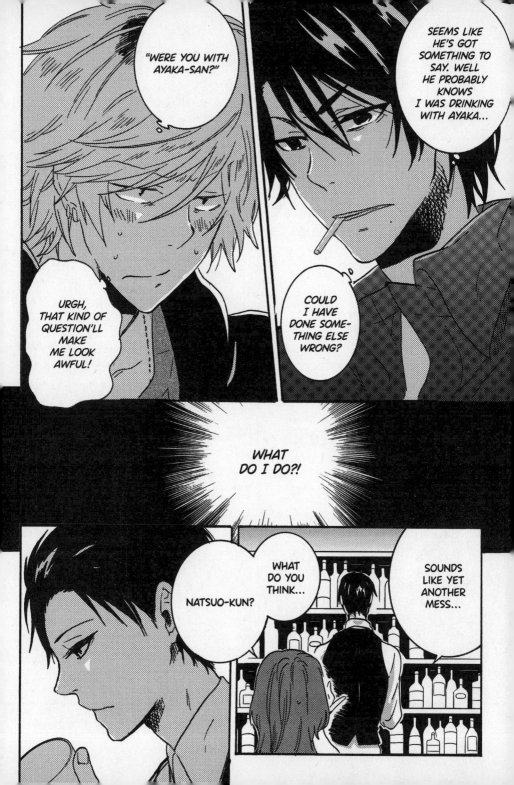

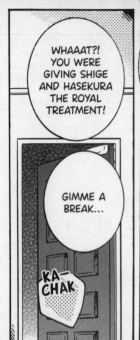

WHAAAT?! YOU WERE GIVING SHIGE AND HASEKURA THE ROYAL TREATMENT!

GIMME A BREAK...

KA-CHAK

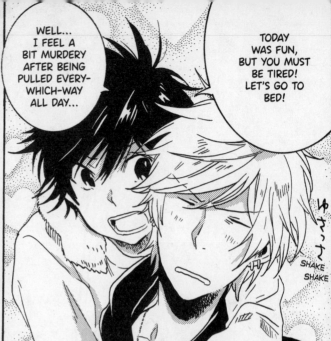

WELL... I FEEL A BIT MURDERY AFTER BEING PULLED EVERY-WHICH-WAY ALL DAY...

TODAY WAS FUN, BUT YOU MUST BE TIRED! LET'S GO TO BED!

SHAKE SHAKE

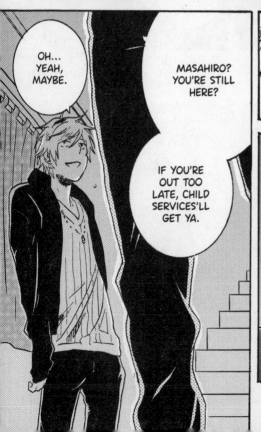

OH... YEAH, MAYBE.

MASAHIRO? YOU'RE STILL HERE?

IF YOU'RE OUT TOO LATE, CHILD SERVICES'LL GET YA.

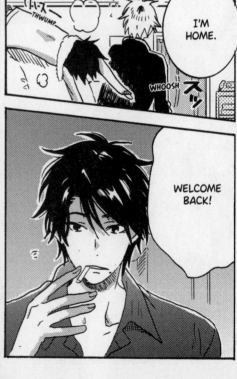

THWUMP

WHOOSH

I'M HOME.

WELCOME BACK!

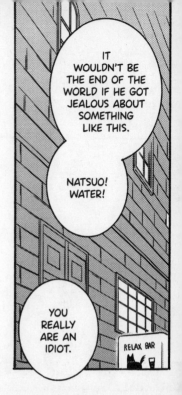

IT WOULDN'T BE THE END OF THE WORLD IF HE GOT JEALOUS ABOUT SOMETHING LIKE THIS.

NATSUO! WATER!

YOU REALLY ARE AN IDIOT.

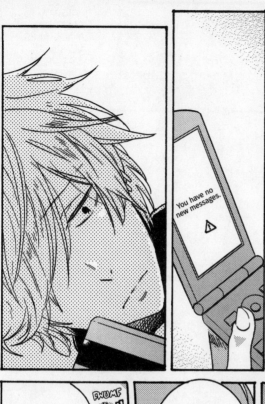

You have no new messages.

AW, C'MON! SPEND THE NIGHT!

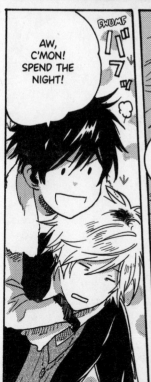

...I THINK I'M JUST ABOUT... TO GO HOME.

OH, REAL-LY?

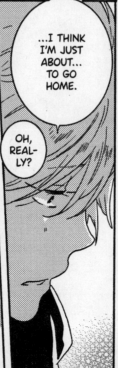

OH, NO!

ARE YOU STAYING OVER, SETAGAWA?

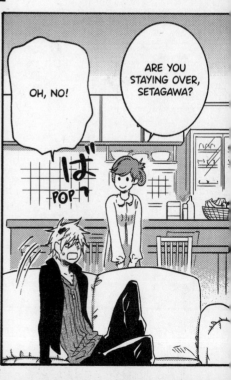

YOU TWO NEED TO PACE YOUR-SELVES.

NATSUOOO! AYAKA'S SAYING SCARY THINGS!

...OR YOU'RE SO SCARED TO BREAK IT YOU LOSE IT BEFORE EVEN TOUCHING IT.

YOU EITHER TAKE SUCH GOOD CARE YOU BREAK IT BY FIDDLING WITH IT...

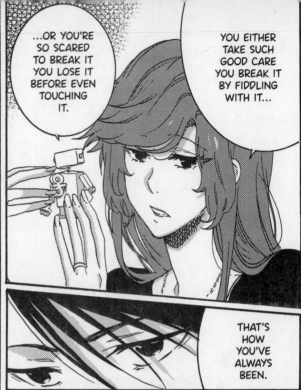

AW, HOW CUTE.

THAT'S HOW YOU'VE ALWAYS BEEN.

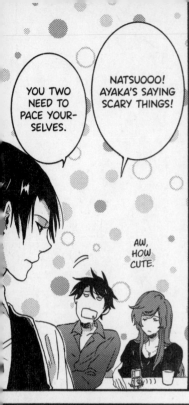

LIKE THAT YOU AND I WENT OUT DRINKING, JUST THE TWO OF US!

BECAUSE NATSUO-KUN'S HERE, TOO, OKAY?

HUNH?

DON'T SAY THINGS TO MAKE THAT BOY HATE ME.

LIKE WHAT?

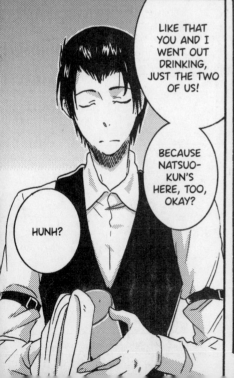

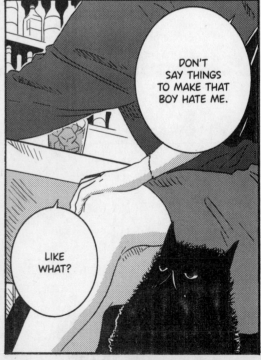

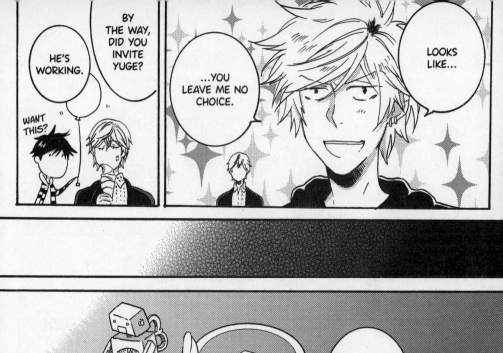

HE'S WORKING.

BY THE WAY, DID YOU INVITE YUGE?

WANT THIS?

...YOU LEAVE ME NO CHOICE.

LOOKS LIKE...

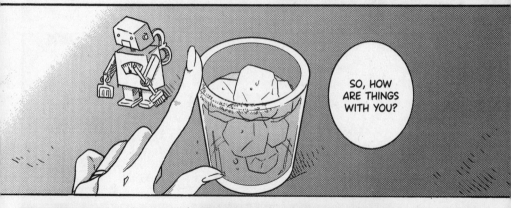

SO, HOW ARE THINGS WITH YOU?

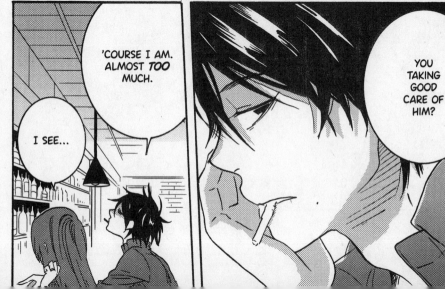

'COURSE I AM. ALMOST *TOO* MUCH.

I SEE...

YOU TAKING GOOD CARE OF HIM?

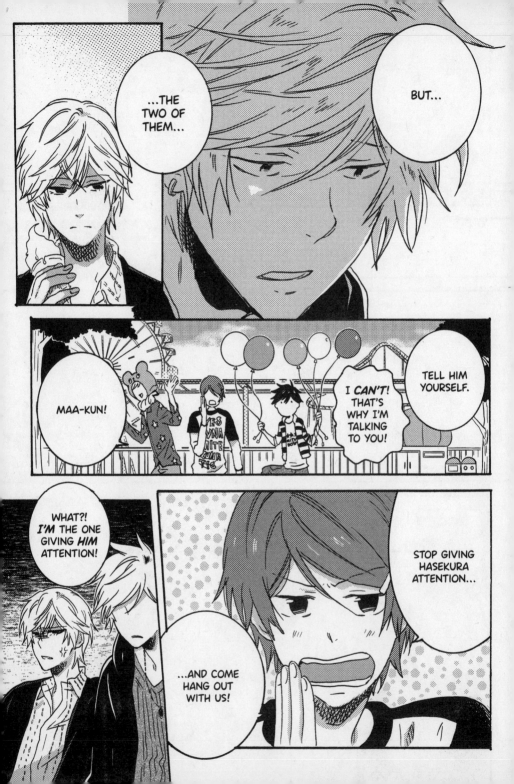

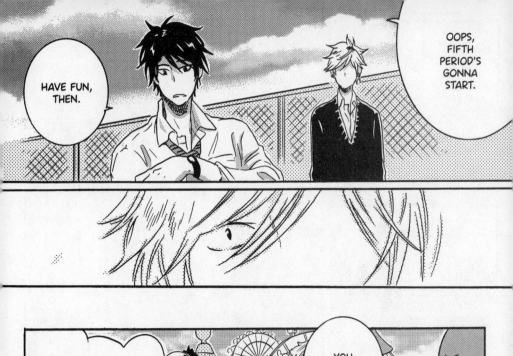

HAVE FUN, THEN.

OOPS, FIFTH PERIOD'S GONNA START.

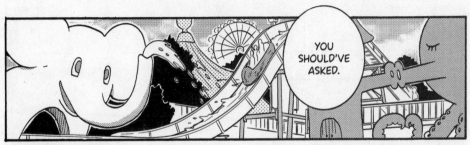

YOU SHOULD'VE ASKED.

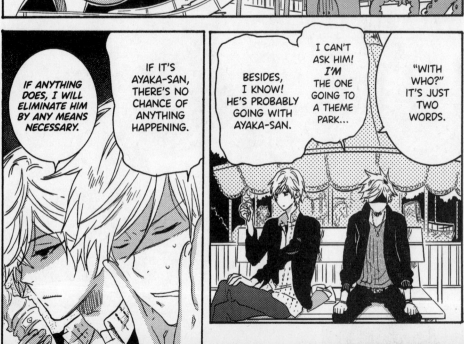

IF ANYTHING DOES, I WILL ELIMINATE HIM BY ANY MEANS NECESSARY.

IF IT'S AYAKA-SAN, THERE'S NO CHANCE OF ANYTHING HAPPENING.

BESIDES, I KNOW! HE'S PROBABLY GOING WITH AYAKA-SAN.

I CAN'T ASK HIM! *I'M* THE ONE GOING TO A THEME PARK...

"WITH WHO?" IT'S JUST TWO WORDS.

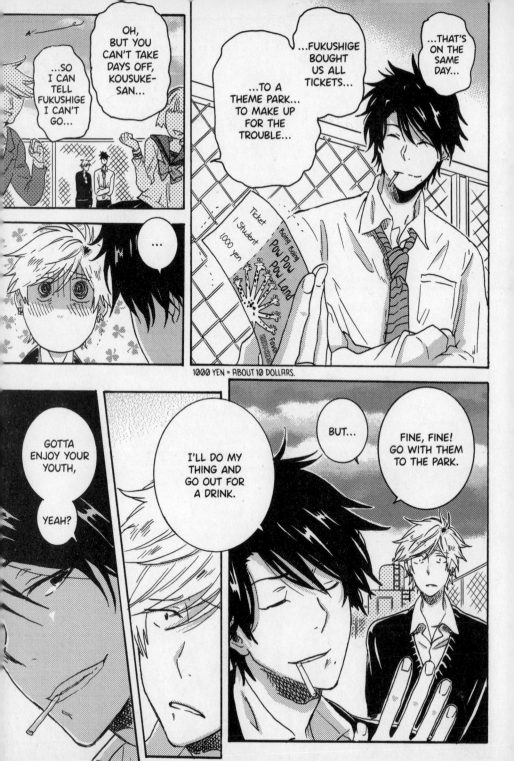

1000 YEN = ABOUT 10 DOLLARS.

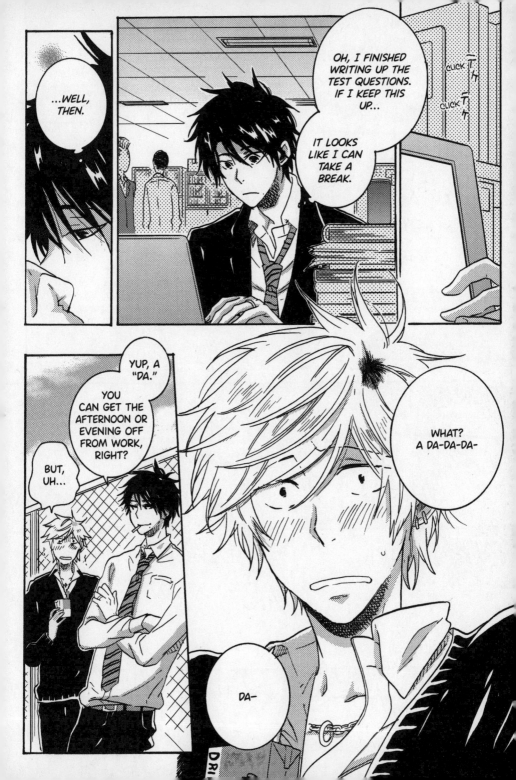

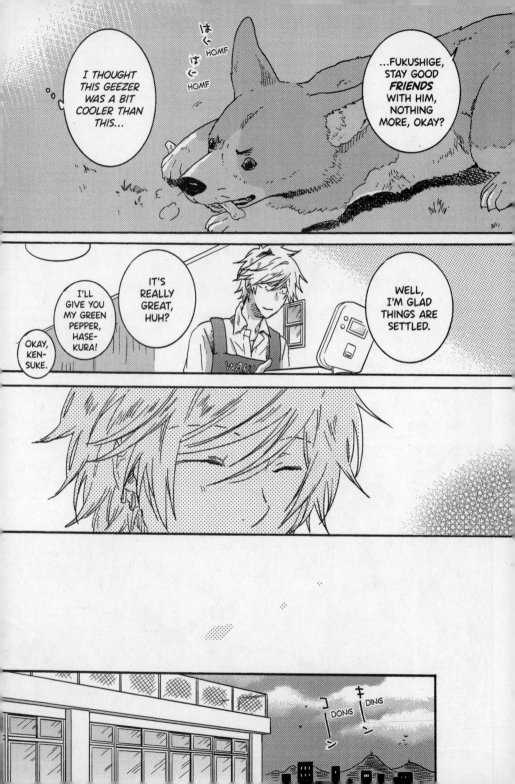

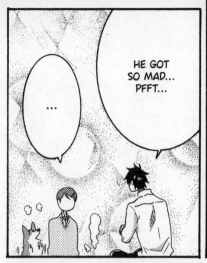

HE GOT SO MAD... PFFT...

...

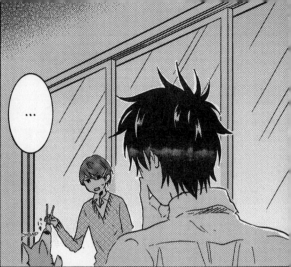

...

CHOMP

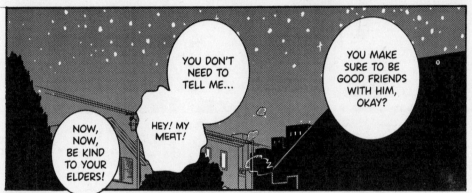

YOU DON'T NEED TO TELL ME...

YOU MAKE SURE TO BE GOOD FRIENDS WITH HIM, OKAY?

HEY! MY MEAT!

NOW, NOW, BE KIND TO YOUR ELDERS!

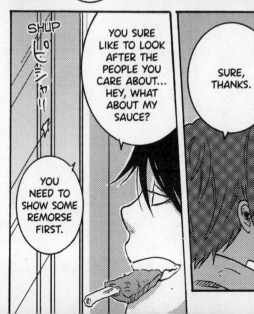

SHUP

YOU SURE LIKE TO LOOK AFTER THE PEOPLE YOU CARE ABOUT... HEY, WHAT ABOUT MY SAUCE?

YOU NEED TO SHOW SOME REMORSE FIRST.

SURE, THANKS.

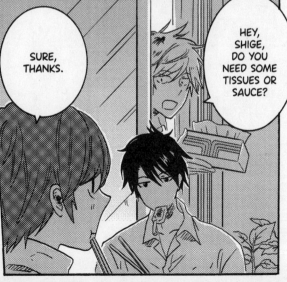

HEY, SHIGE, DO YOU NEED SOME TISSUES OR SAUCE?

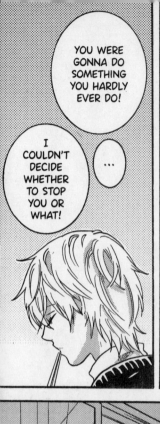

YOU WERE GONNA DO SOMETHING YOU HARDLY EVER DO!

I COULDN'T DECIDE WHETHER TO STOP YOU OR WHAT!

...

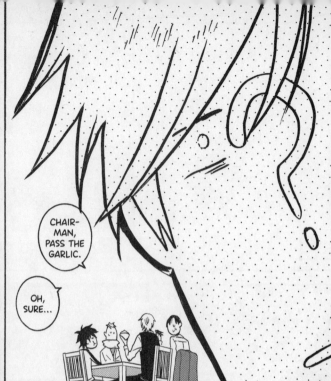

CHAIR-MAN, PASS THE GARLIC.

OH, SURE...

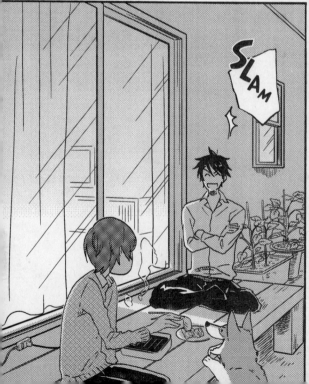

SLAM

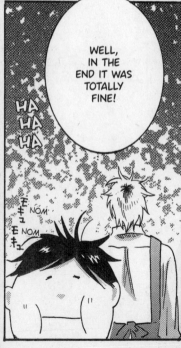

WELL, IN THE END IT WAS TOTALLY FINE!

HA HA HA

NOM NOM

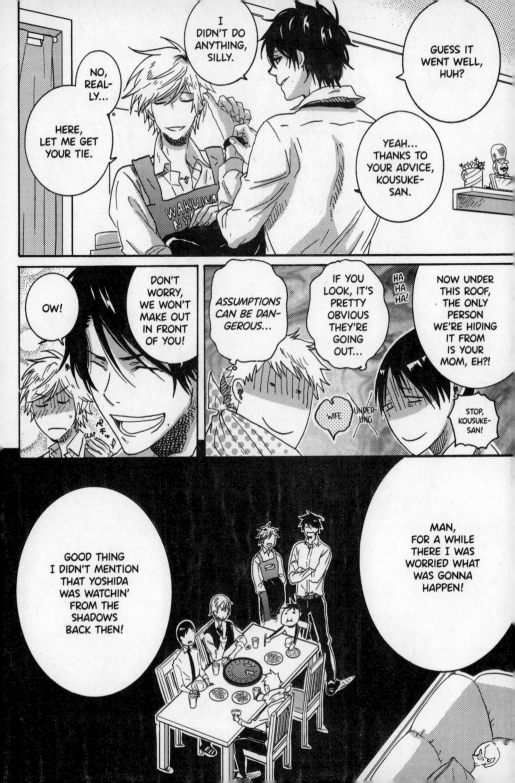

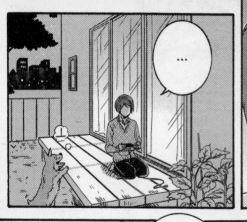

...

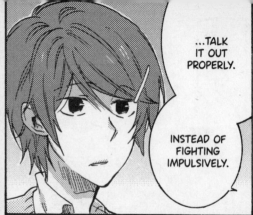

...TALK IT OUT PROPERLY.

INSTEAD OF FIGHTING IMPULSIVELY.

NOW LET'S GET COOKIN'!

WOO!

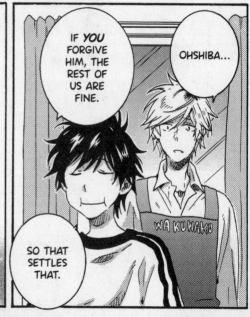

OHSHIBA...

IF *YOU* FORGIVE HIM, THE REST OF US ARE FINE.

SO THAT SETTLES THAT.

WA KU WAKU

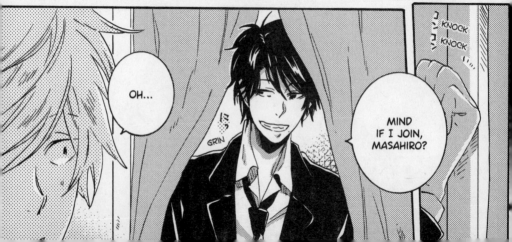

OH...

GRIN

KNOCK KNOCK

MIND IF I JOIN, MASAHIRO?

WHAT'RE YOU DOIN' AT OUR DOORSTEP? YOU'RE BANISHED, YOU KNOW.

H-HEY! DON'T YOU THINK THAT'S A BIT HARSH...?

AND THAT TAKES CARE OF THAT.

SLAM

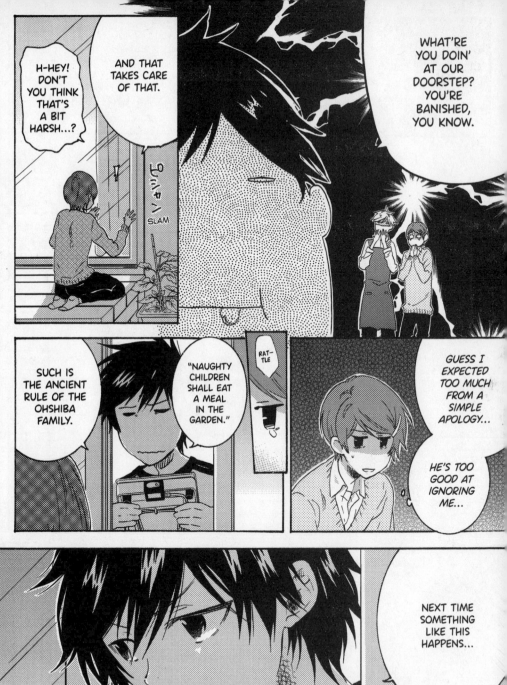

SUCH IS THE ANCIENT RULE OF THE OHSHIBA FAMILY.

"NAUGHTY CHILDREN SHALL EAT A MEAL IN THE GARDEN."

RAT- TLE

GUESS I EXPECTED TOO MUCH FROM A SIMPLE APOLOGY...

HE'S TOO GOOD AT IGNORING ME...

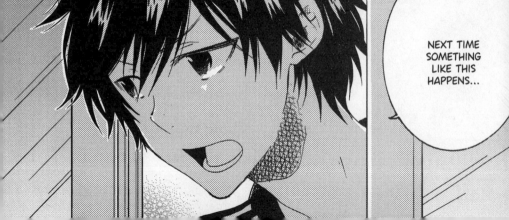

NEXT TIME SOMETHING LIKE THIS HAPPENS...

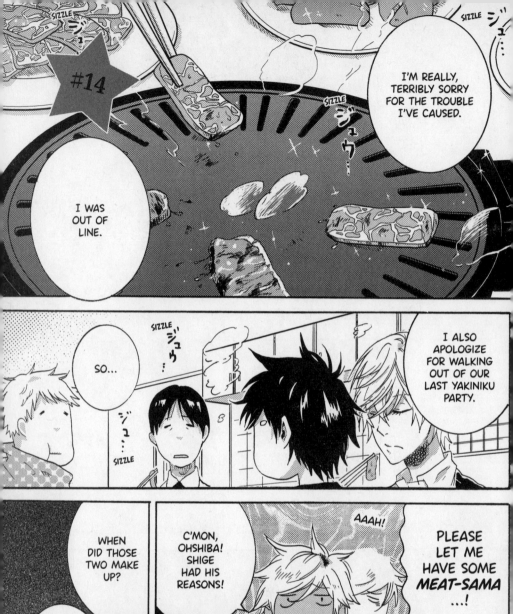

#14

I'M REALLY, TERRIBLY SORRY FOR THE TROUBLE I'VE CAUSED.

I WAS OUT OF LINE.

SO...

I ALSO APOLOGIZE FOR WALKING OUT OF OUR LAST YAKINIKU PARTY.

SIZZLE

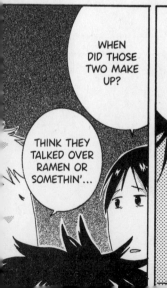

WHEN DID THOSE TWO MAKE UP?

THINK THEY TALKED OVER RAMEN OR SOMETHIN'...

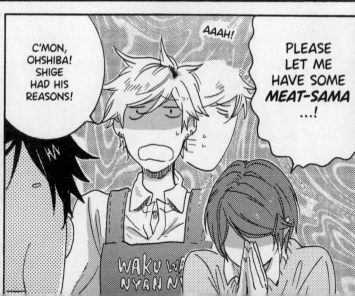

C'MON, OHSHIBA! SHIGE HAD HIS REASONS!

AAAH!

PLEASE LET ME HAVE SOME *MEAT-SAMA* ...!

WAKU WA
NYAN N

He's the type to start talking about deep stuff the moment he becomes close to someone.

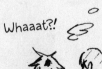

Whaaat?!

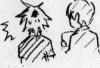

So like, I think my dad's having an affair...

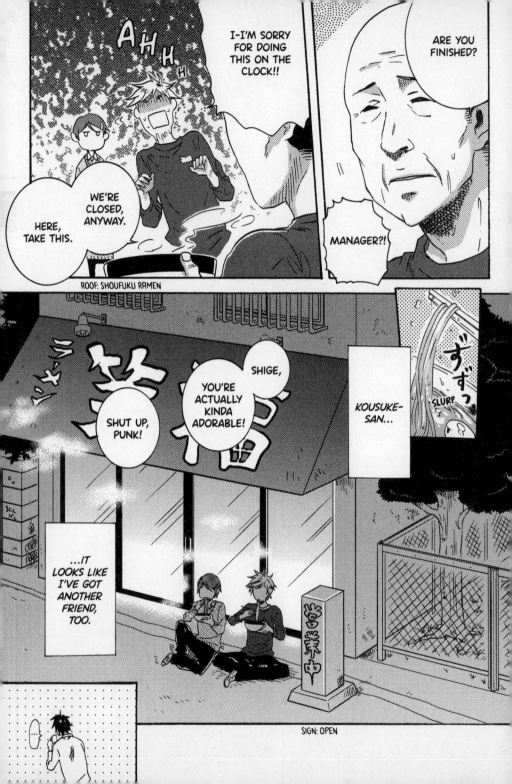

AHHHHH

I-I'M SORRY FOR DOING THIS ON THE CLOCK!!

ARE YOU FINISHED?

WE'RE CLOSED, ANYWAY.

HERE, TAKE THIS.

MANAGER?!

ROOF: SHOUFUKU RAMEN

SLURP

SHIGE, YOU'RE ACTUALLY KINDA ADORABLE!

SHUT UP, PUNK!

KOUSUKE-SAN...

...IT LOOKS LIKE I'VE GOT ANOTHER FRIEND, TOO.

SIGN: OPEN

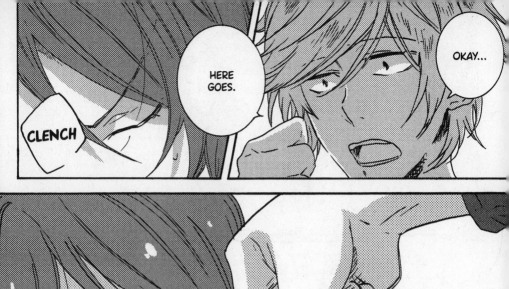

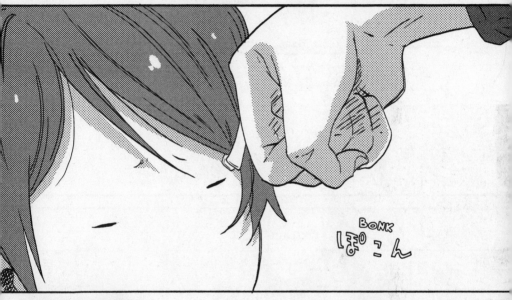

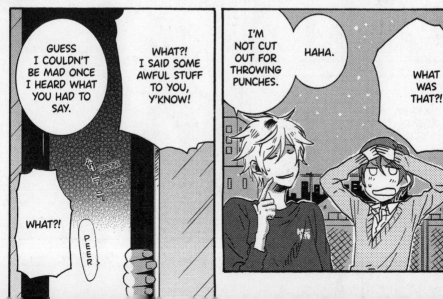

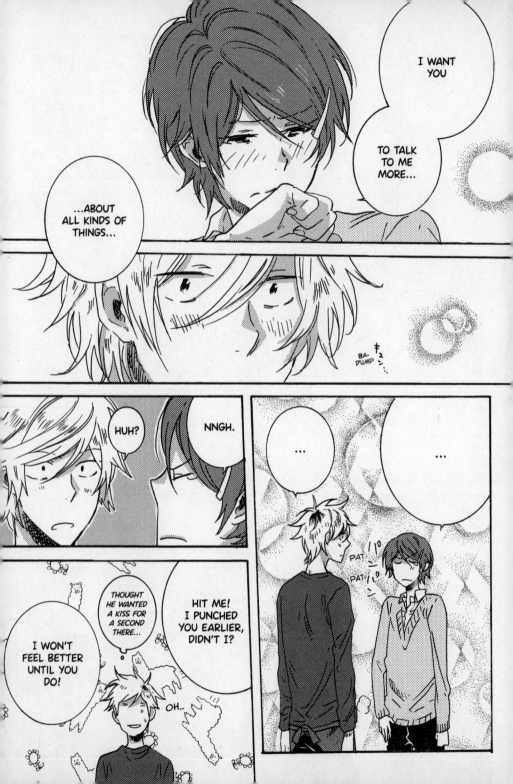

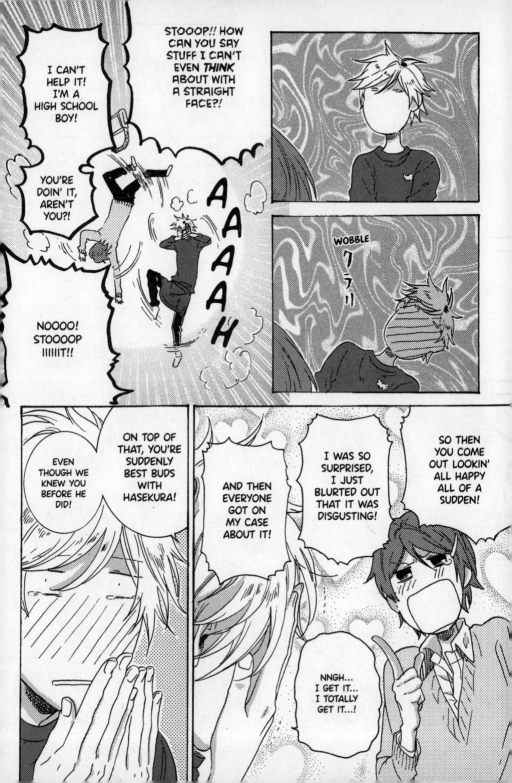

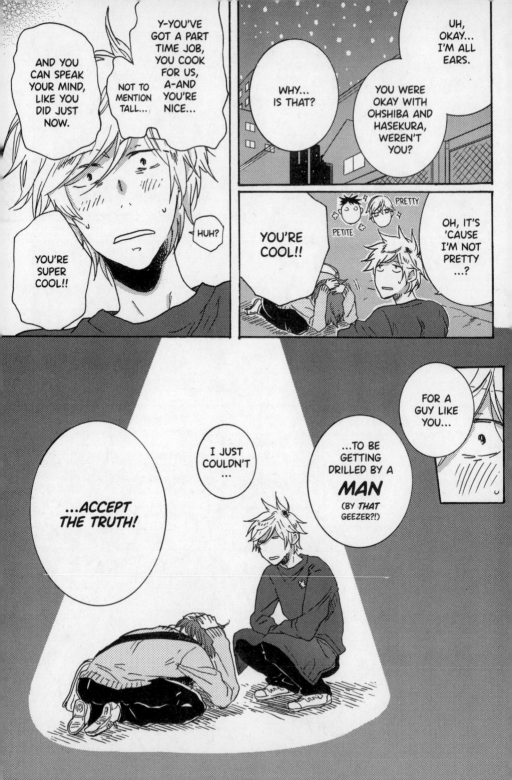

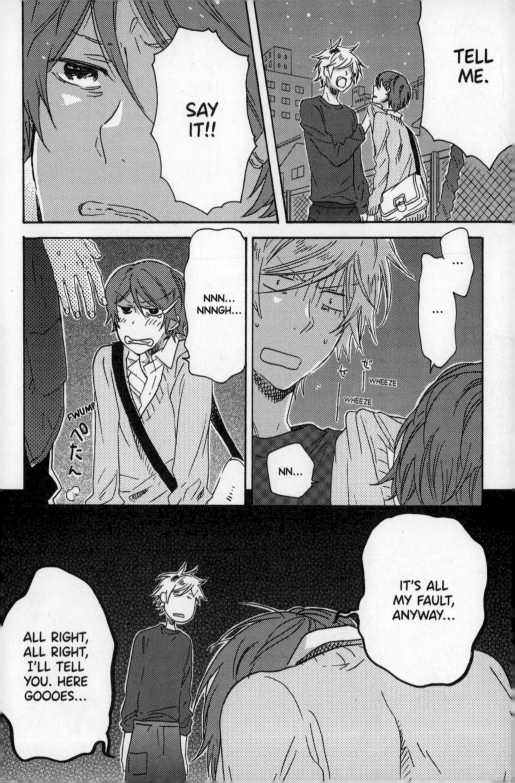

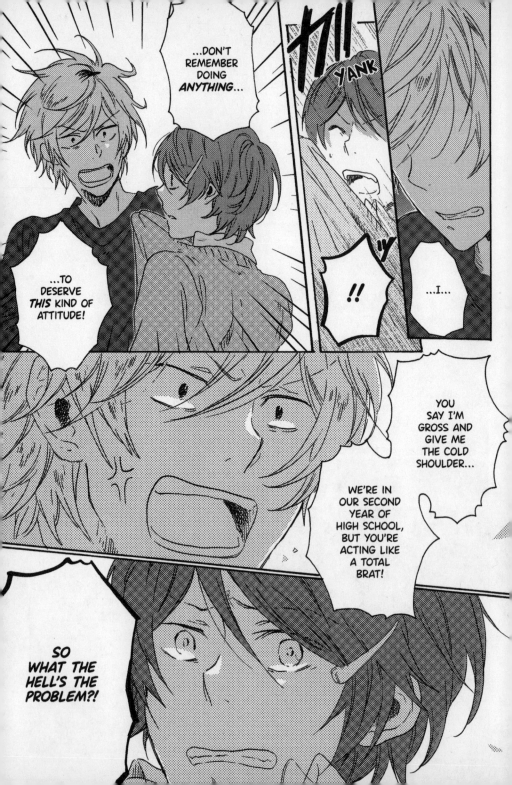

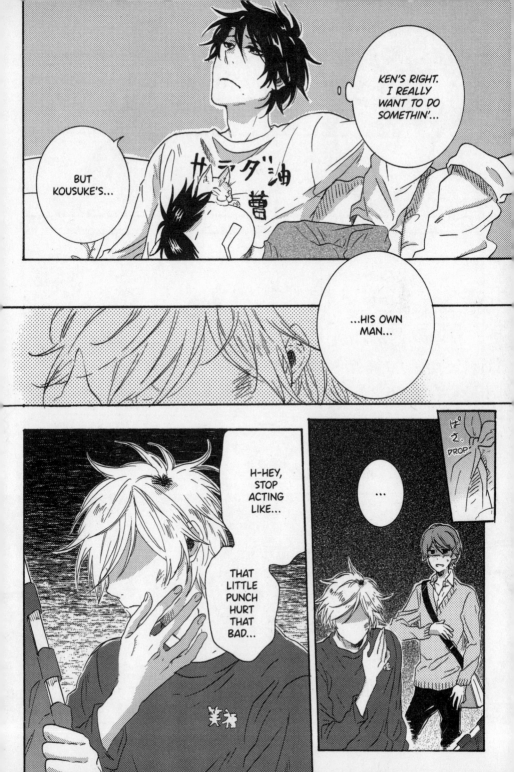

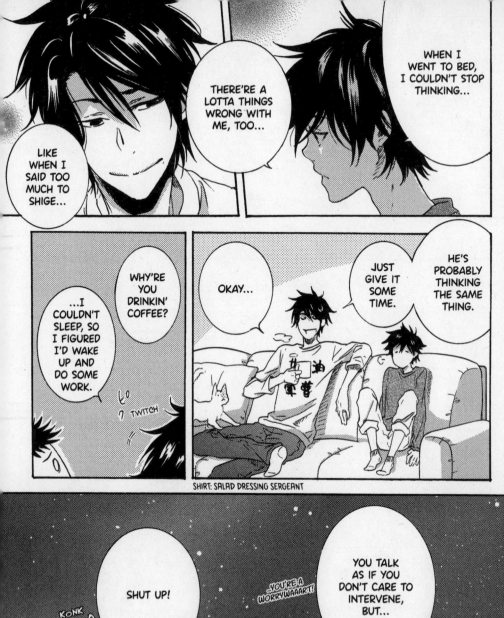

WHEN I WENT TO BED, I COULDN'T STOP THINKING...

THERE'RE A LOTTA THINGS WRONG WITH ME, TOO...

LIKE WHEN I SAID TOO MUCH TO SHIGE...

...I COULDN'T SLEEP, SO I FIGURED I'D WAKE UP AND DO SOME WORK.

WHY'RE YOU DRINKIN' COFFEE?

TWITCH

OKAY...

JUST GIVE IT SOME TIME.

HE'S PROBABLY THINKING THE SAME THING.

SHIRT: SALAD DRESSING SERGEANT

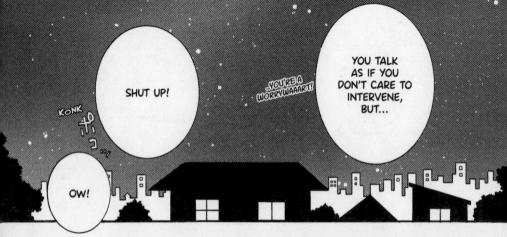

SHUT UP!

...YOU'RE A WORRYWAAART!

KONK

OW!

YOU TALK AS IF YOU DON'T CARE TO INTERVENE, BUT...

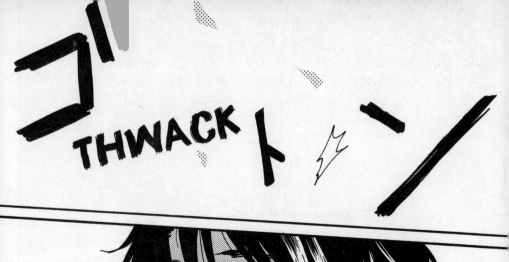

THWACK

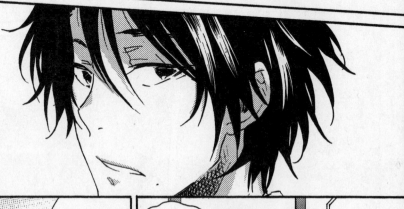

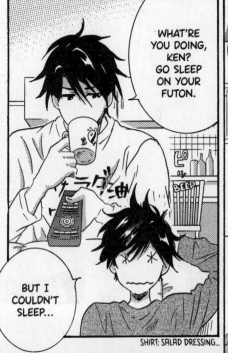

WHAT'RE YOU DOING, KEN? GO SLEEP ON YOUR FUTON.

BUT I COULDN'T SLEEP...

SHIRT: SALAD DRESSING...

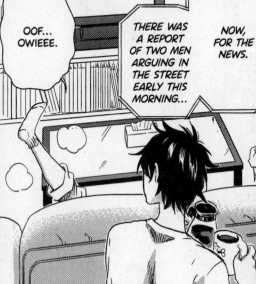

OOF... OWIEEE.

THERE WAS A REPORT OF TWO MEN ARGUING IN THE STREET EARLY THIS MORNING...

NOW, FOR THE NEWS.

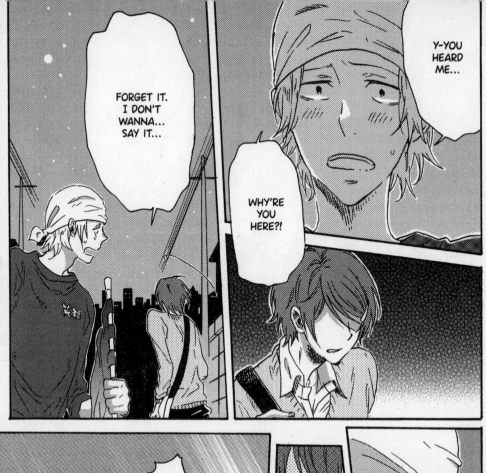

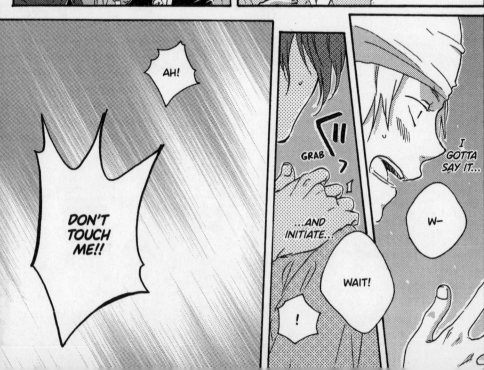

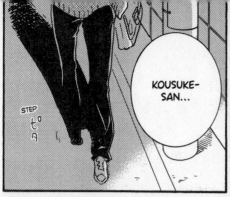

KOUSUKE-SAN...

STEP

I WAS ONLY ABLE TO DO THAT...

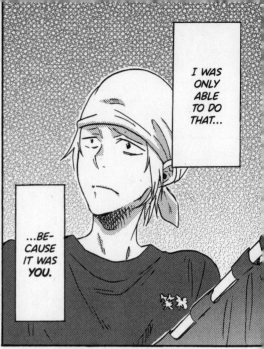

GASP

KOUSUKE-SAN, HUH...?

...BE-CAUSE IT WAS YOU.

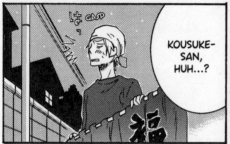

福

FUKU...

SHIGE...

WELL, SORRY I'M NOT HIM.

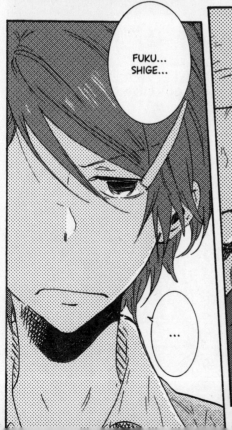

...

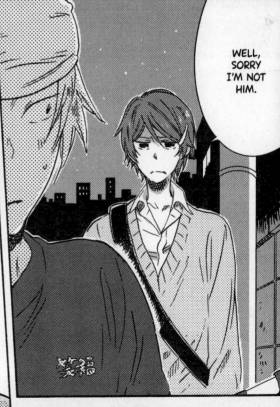

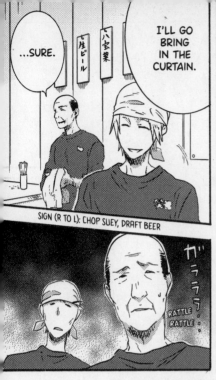

...SURE.

I'LL GO BRING IN THE CURTAIN.

SIGN (R TO L): CHOP SUEY, DRAFT BEER

RATTLE RATTLE

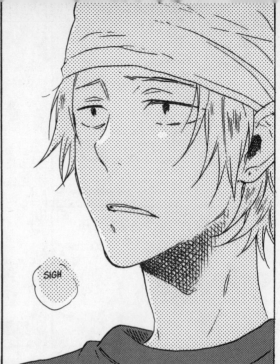

SIGH

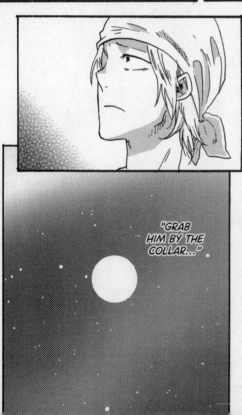

"GRAB HIM BY THE COLLAR..."

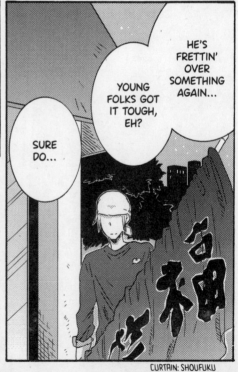

HE'S FRETTIN' OVER SOMETHING AGAIN...

YOUNG FOLKS GOT IT TOUGH, EH?

SURE DO...

CURTAIN: SHOUFUKU

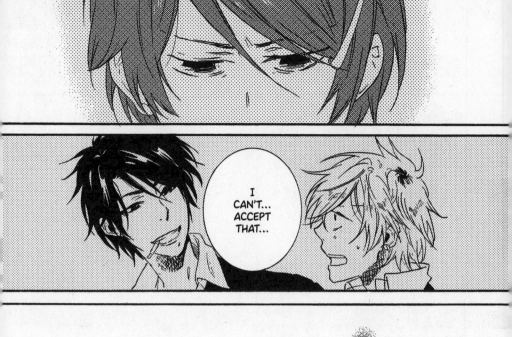

I CAN'T... ACCEPT THAT...

ROOF: SHOUFUKU RAMEN

RATTLE

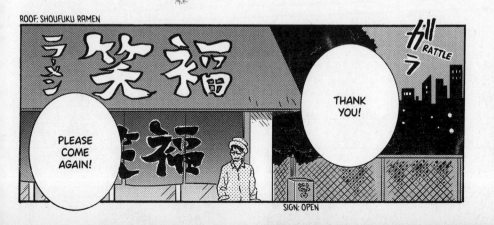

PLEASE COME AGAIN!

THANK YOU!

SIGN: OPEN

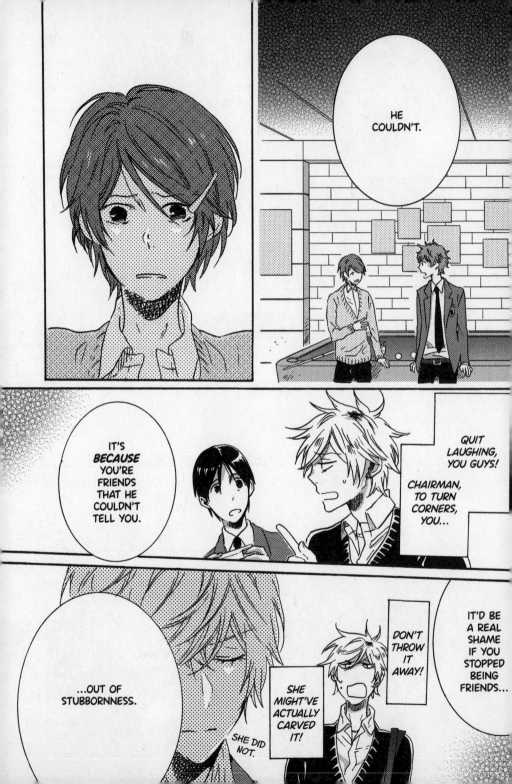

HE COULDN'T.

IT'S *BECAUSE* YOU'RE FRIENDS THAT HE COULDN'T TELL YOU.

QUIT LAUGHING, YOU GUYS!

CHAIRMAN, TO TURN CORNERS, YOU...

...OUT OF STUBBORNNESS.

IT'D BE A REAL SHAME IF YOU STOPPED BEING FRIENDS...

DON'T THROW IT AWAY!

SHE MIGHT'VE ACTUALLY CARVED IT!

SHE DID NOT.

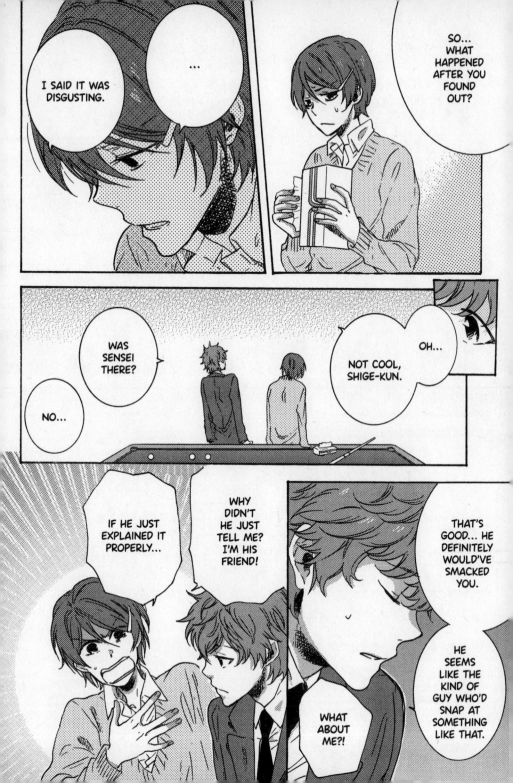

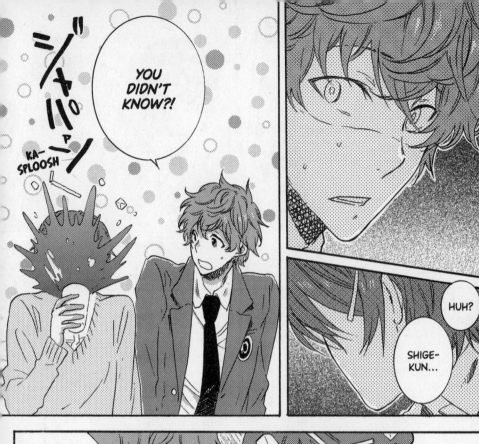

YOU DIDN'T KNOW?!

KA-SPLOOSH

HUH?

SHIGE-KUN...

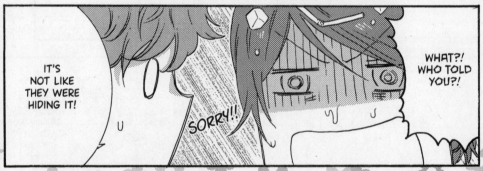

IT'S NOT LIKE THEY WERE HIDING IT!

SORRY!!

WHAT?! WHO TOLD YOU?!

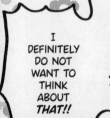

I DEFINITELY DO NOT WANT TO THINK ABOUT *THAT!!*

STOP! STOP! STOP! STOP!!

...NOT TO MENTION THE CHEMISTRY...

ALWAYS IN A LOVEY-DOVEY BUBBLE...

MAYBE THEY DON'T SHOW IT AT SCHOOL, BUT THEY'RE SUPER CLOSE WHEN THEY'RE AT THE HOUSE!

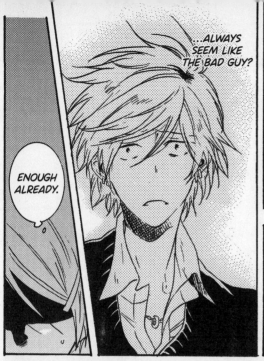

...ALWAYS SEEM LIKE THE BAD GUY?

ENOUGH ALREADY.

NO ONE'S ON MY SIDE.

...THE ONE WHO WON'T EMBRACE THINGS!!

WHY DOES!...

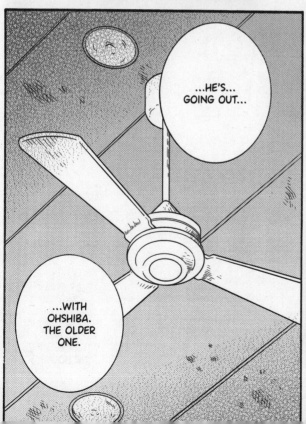

...HE'S... GOING OUT...

...WITH OHSHIBA. THE OLDER ONE.

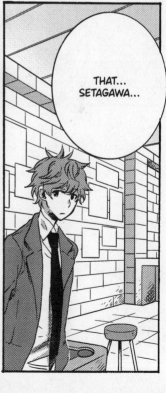

THAT... SETAGAWA...

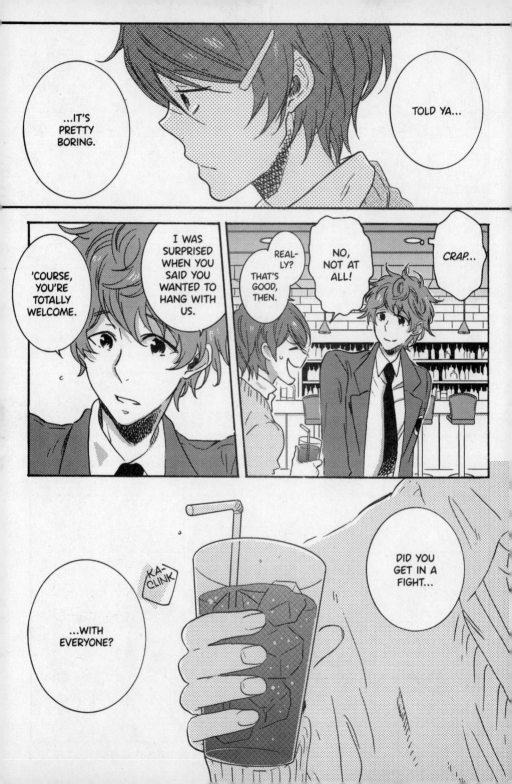

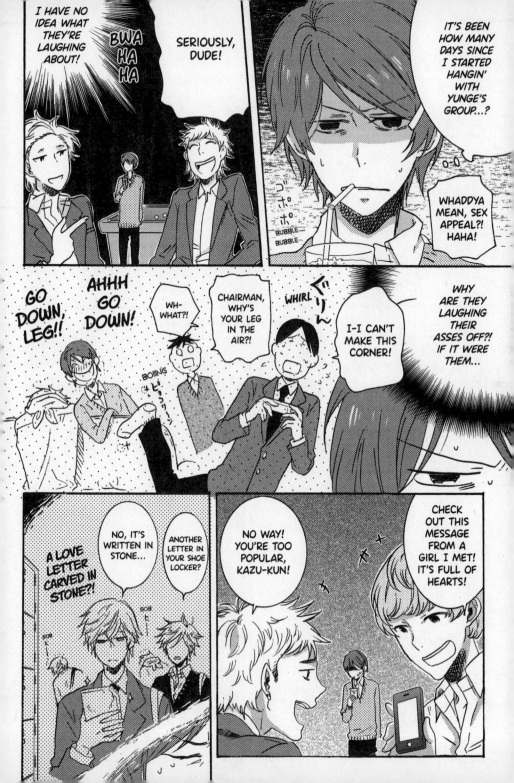

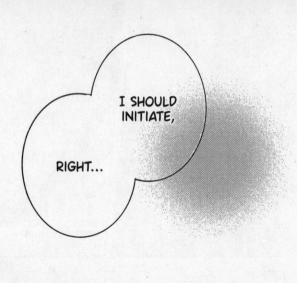

I SHOULD INITIATE,

RIGHT...

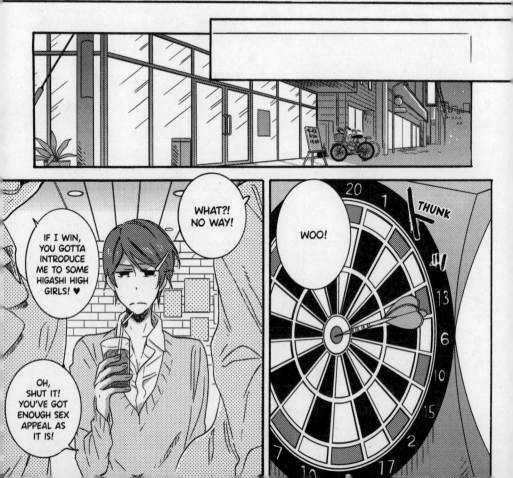

IF I WIN, YOU GOTTA INTRODUCE ME TO SOME HIGASHI HIGH GIRLS! ♥

WHAT?! NO WAY!

WOO!

THUNK

OH, SHUT IT! YOU'VE GOT ENOUGH SEX APPEAL AS IT IS!

20 1

13

6

10

15

2

17

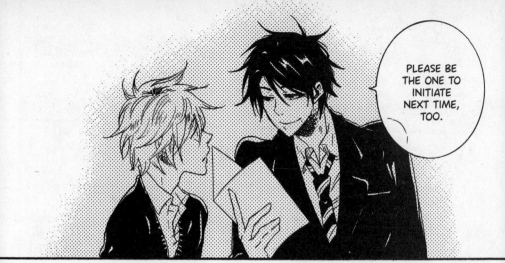

PLEASE BE THE ONE TO INITIATE NEXT TIME, TOO.

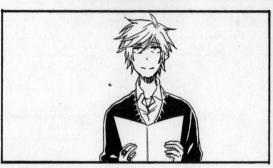

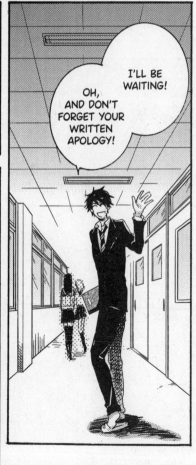

I'LL BE WAITING!

OH, AND DON'T FORGET YOUR WRITTEN APOLOGY!

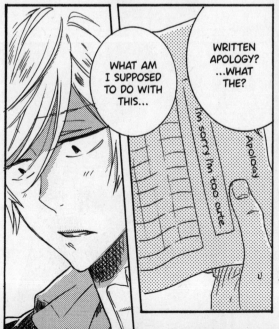

WHAT AM I SUPPOSED TO DO WITH THIS...

WRITTEN APOLOGY? ...WHAT THE?

I'm sorry I'm too cute.

Apology

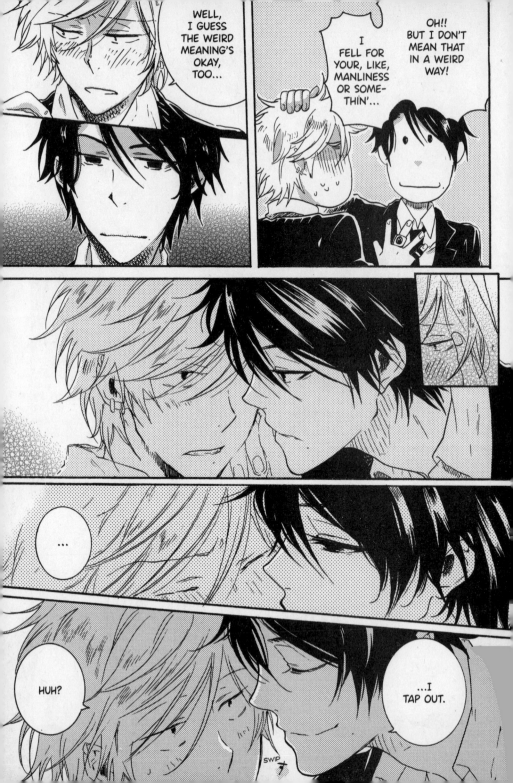

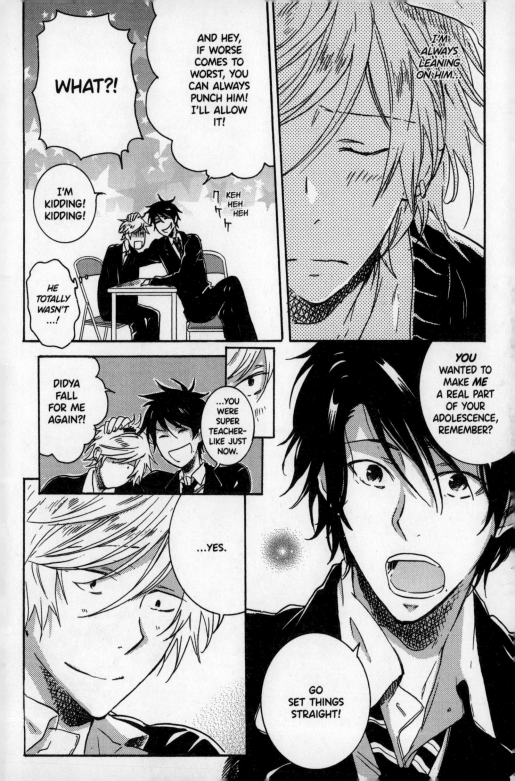

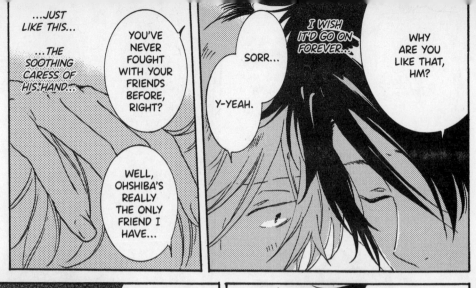

...JUST LIKE THIS...

...THE SOOTHING CARESS OF HIS HAND...

YOU'VE NEVER FOUGHT WITH YOUR FRIENDS BEFORE, RIGHT?

WELL, OHSHIBA'S REALLY THE ONLY FRIEND I HAVE...

SORR...

Y-YEAH.

I WISH IT'D GO ON FOREVER...

WHY ARE YOU LIKE THAT, HM?

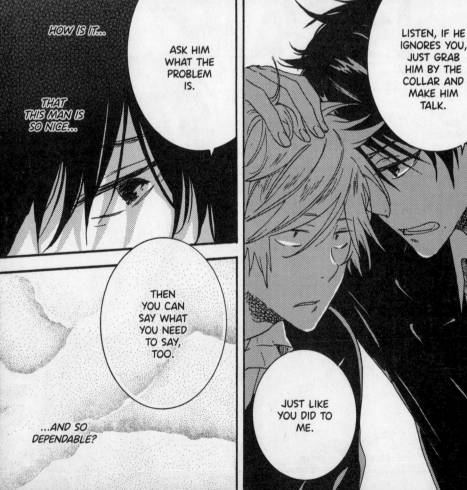

HOW IS IT...

THAT THIS MAN IS SO NICE...

ASK HIM WHAT THE PROBLEM IS.

THEN YOU CAN SAY WHAT YOU NEED TO SAY, TOO.

...AND SO DEPENDABLE?

LISTEN, IF HE IGNORES YOU, JUST GRAB HIM BY THE COLLAR AND MAKE HIM TALK.

JUST LIKE YOU DID TO ME.

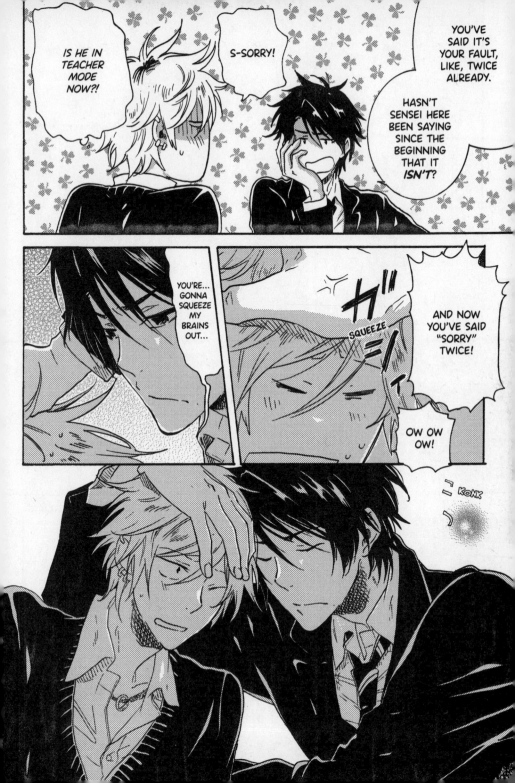

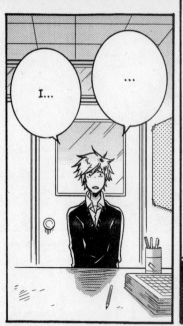

I...

...

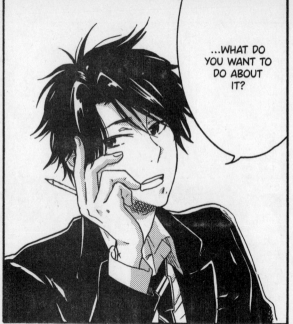

...WHAT DO YOU WANT TO DO ABOUT IT?

BUT HE KEEPS BLOWING ME OFF. IT'S NOT LIKE I CAN FORCE HIM TO TALK TO ME.

...NO ONE'S

GETTING ALONG ANYMORE BECAUSE OF ME.

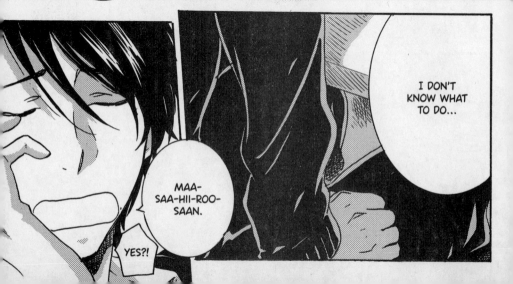

I DON'T KNOW WHAT TO DO...

MAA-SAA-HII-ROO-SAAN.

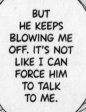

YES?!

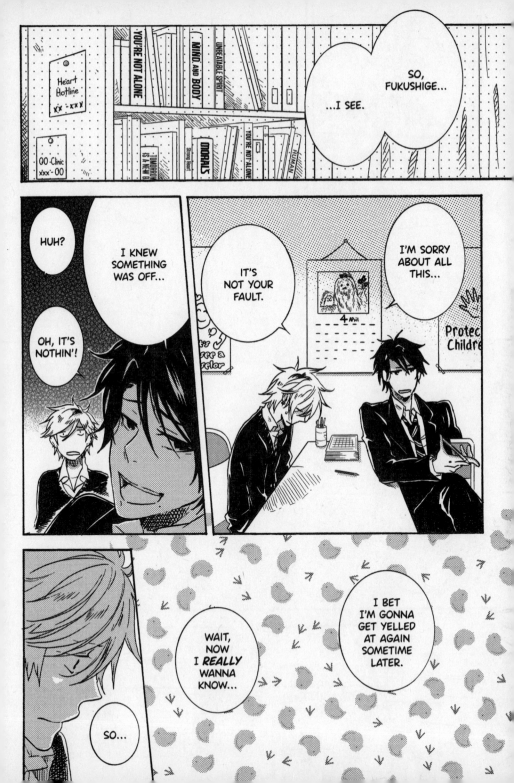

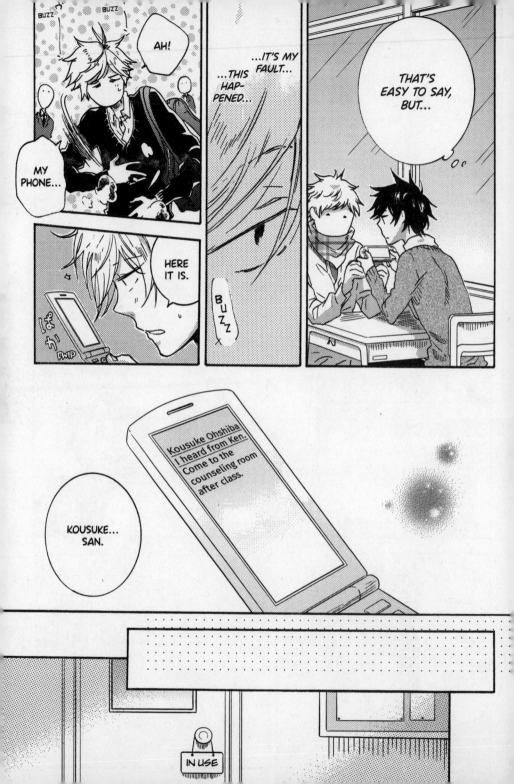

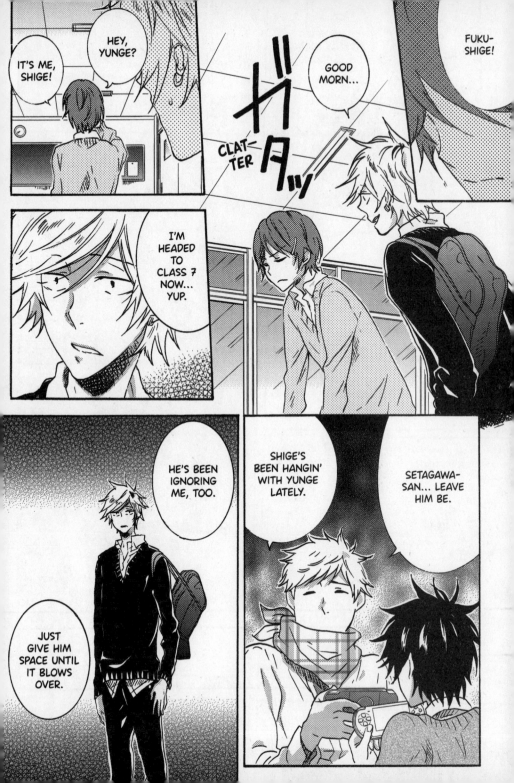

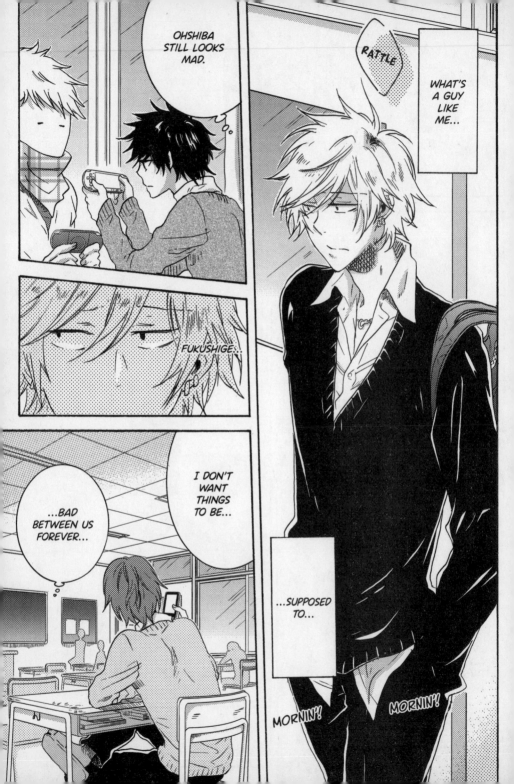

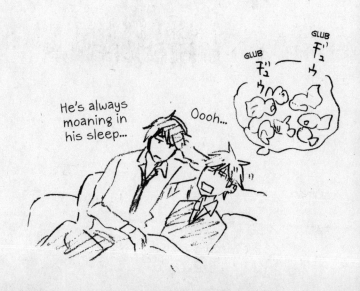

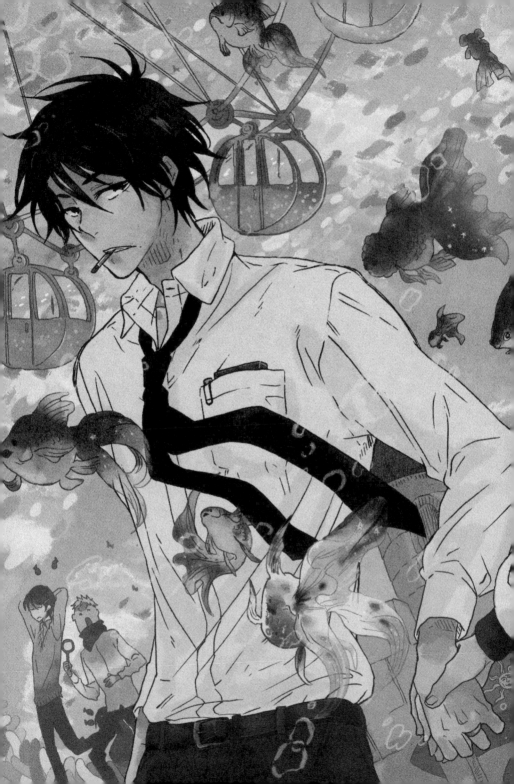

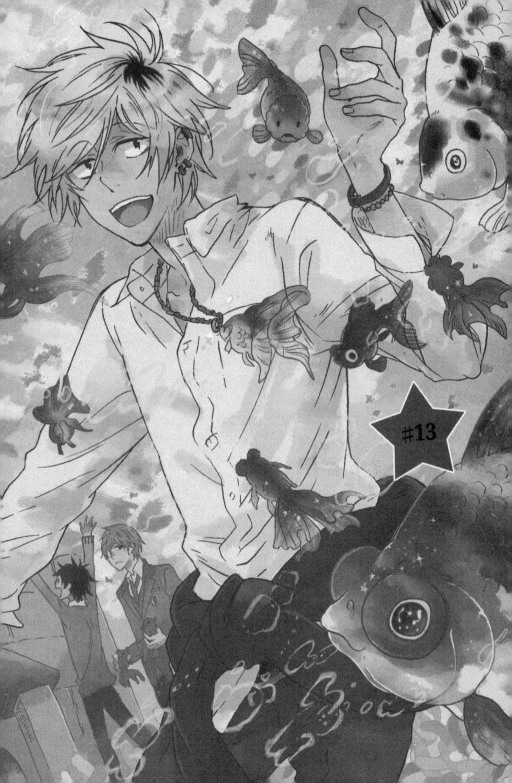

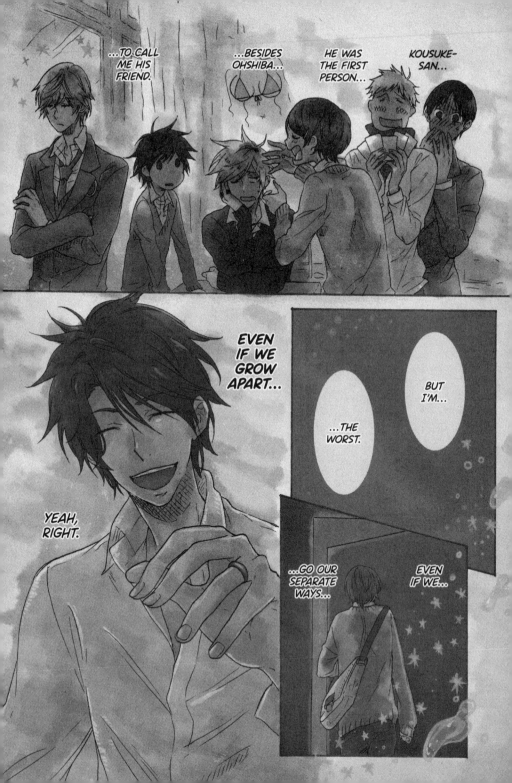

Hitorijime
My Hero

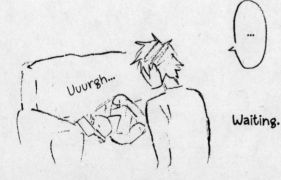

Uuurgh...

...

Waiting.

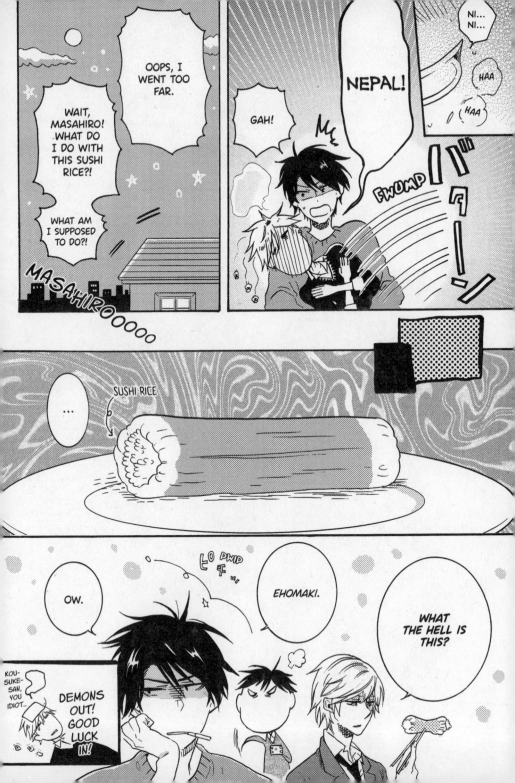

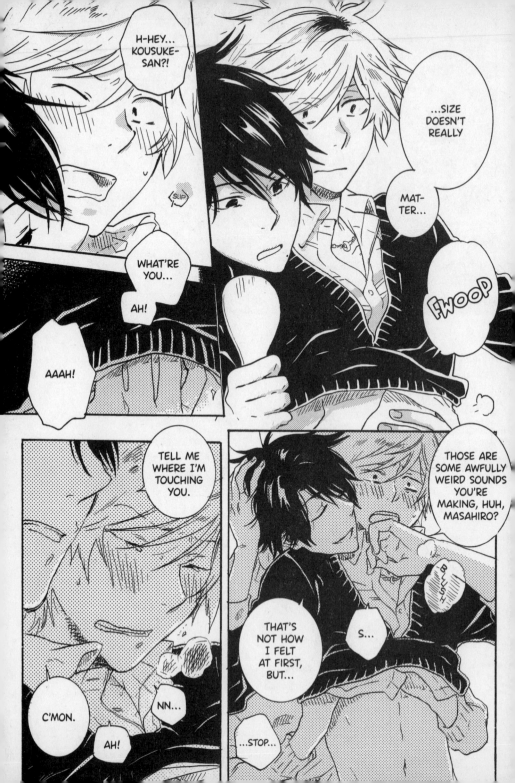

...

SUSHI RICE

WELL...

...I SUPPOSE BIGGER IS BETTER.

A-ANSWER THE QUESTION!

GULP

WHAT? IS THIS ABOUT KAIDE-SENSEI?

I THOUGHT I SAW YOU STARING.

SULK

SULK

SULK

I KNEW IT.

BUT...

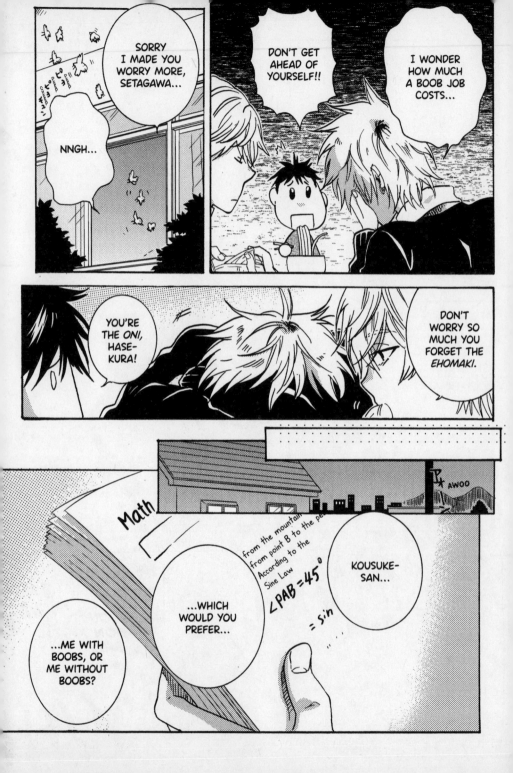

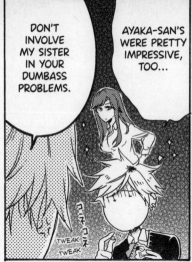

DON'T INVOLVE MY SISTER IN YOUR DUMBASS PROBLEMS.

AYAKA-SAN'S WERE PRETTY IMPRESSIVE, TOO...

TWEAK
TWEAK

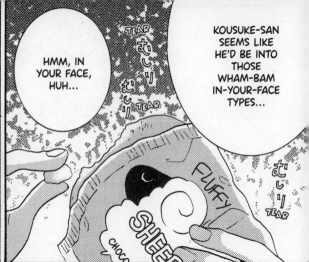

HMM, IN YOUR FACE, HUH...

KOUSUKE-SAN SEEMS LIKE HE'D BE INTO THOSE WHAM-BAM IN-YOUR-FACE TYPES...

TEAR

FLUFFY

SHEE

CHOCO

TEAR

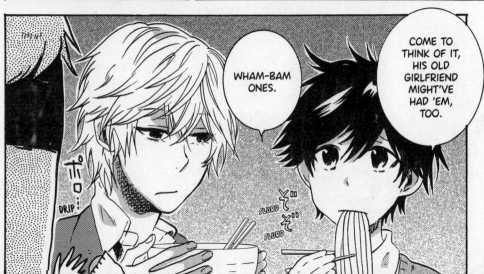

WHAM-BAM ONES.

COME TO THINK OF IT, HIS OLD GIRLFRIEND MIGHT'VE HAD 'EM, TOO.

DRIP

SLURP
SLURP

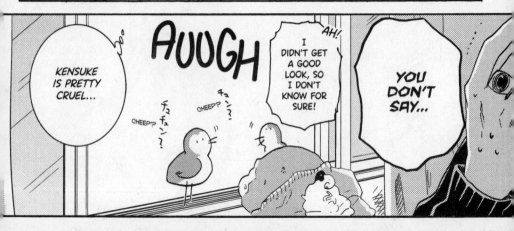

KENSUKE IS PRETTY CRUEL...

AUUGH

AH! I DIDN'T GET A GOOD LOOK, SO I DON'T KNOW FOR SURE!

YOU DON'T SAY...

CHEEP?

CHEEP?

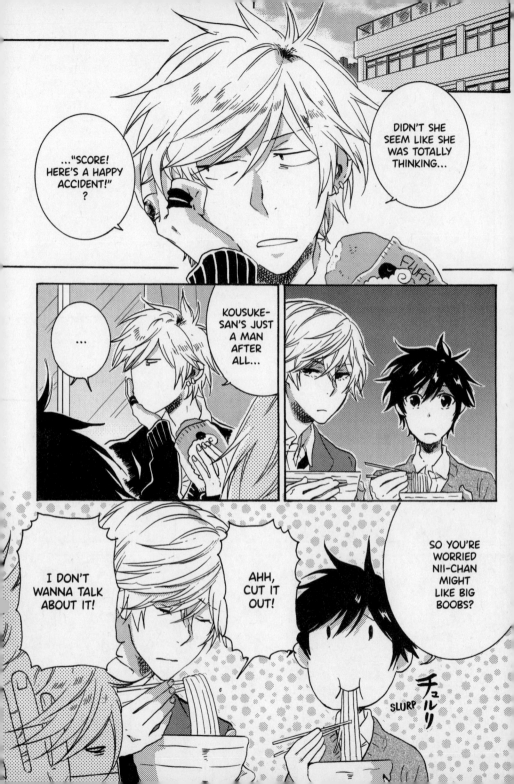

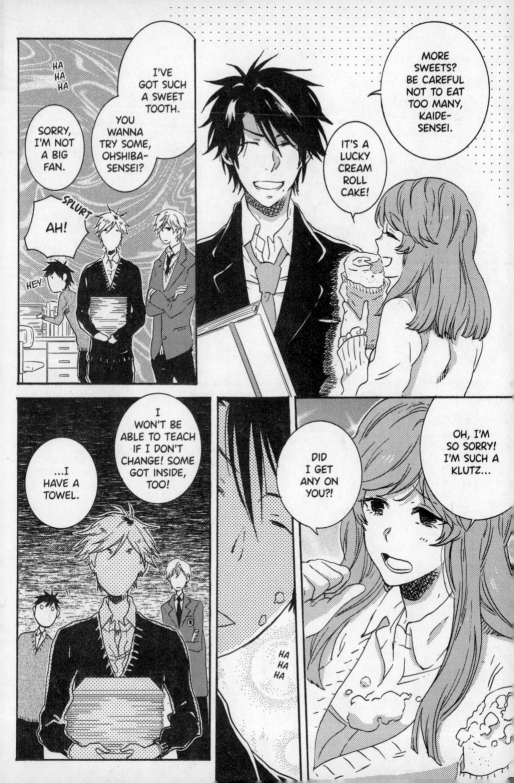

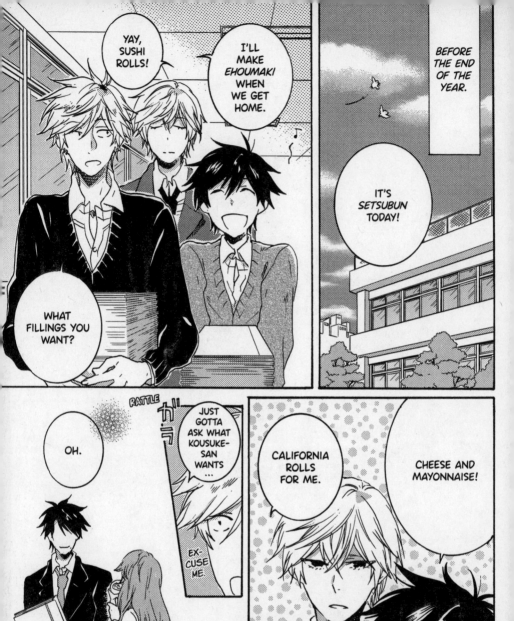

Hitorijime
My Hero

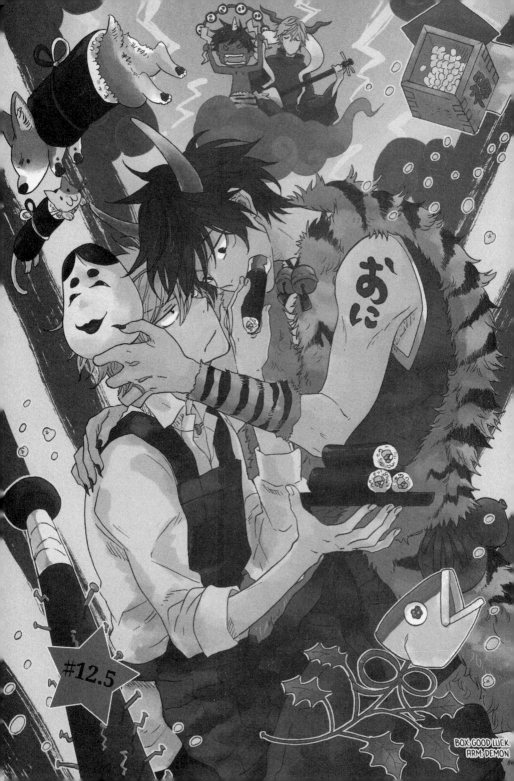

#12.5

BOX: GOOD LUCK
ARM: DEMON

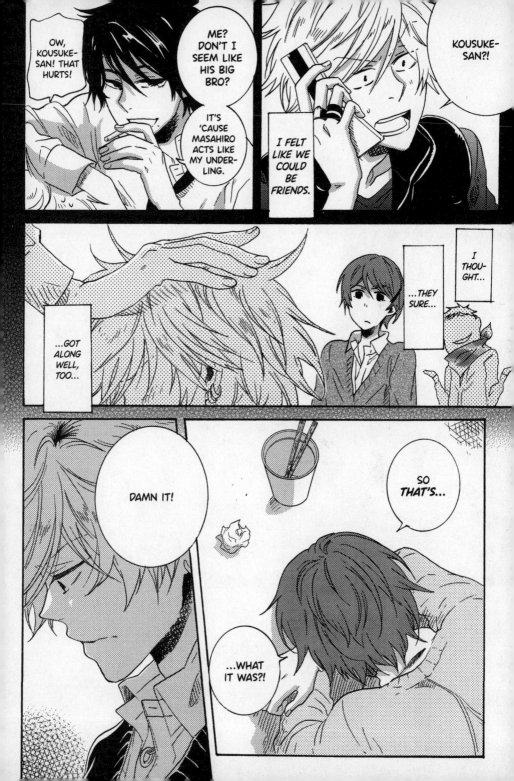

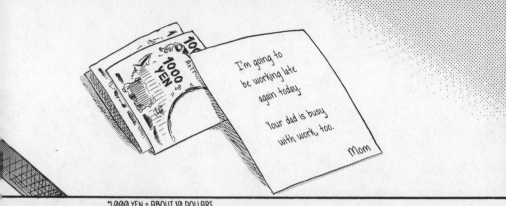

I'm going to be working late again today.

Your dad is busy with work, too.

Mom

*1,000 YEN = ABOUT 10 DOLLARS.

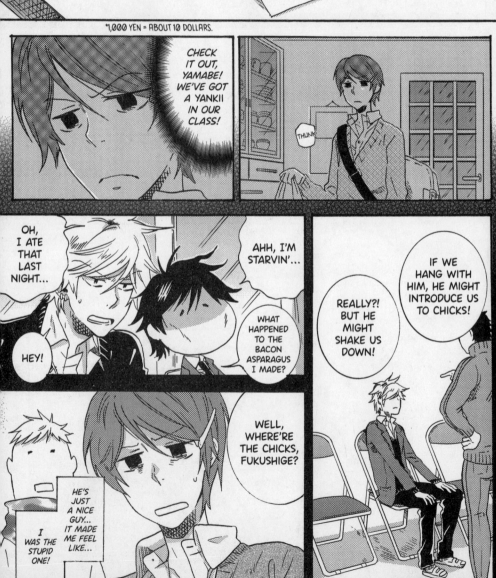

CHECK IT OUT, YAMABE! WE'VE GOT A YANKII IN OUR CLASS!

THUNK

OH, I ATE THAT LAST NIGHT...

HEY!

AHH, I'M STARVIN'...

WHAT HAPPENED TO THE BACON ASPARAGUS I MADE?

REALLY?! BUT HE MIGHT SHAKE US DOWN!

IF WE HANG WITH HIM, HE MIGHT INTRODUCE US TO CHICKS!

WELL, WHERE'RE THE CHICKS, FUKUSHIGE?

I WAS THE STUPID ONE!

HE'S JUST A NICE GUY... IT MADE ME FEEL LIKE...

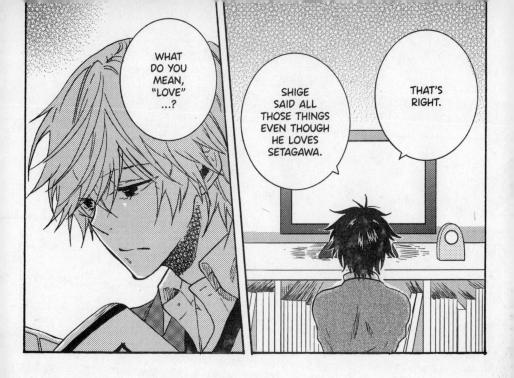

WHAT DO YOU MEAN, "LOVE" ...?

SHIGE SAID ALL THOSE THINGS EVEN THOUGH HE LOVES SETAGAWA.

THAT'S RIGHT.

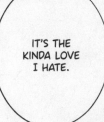

IT'S THE KINDA LOVE I HATE.

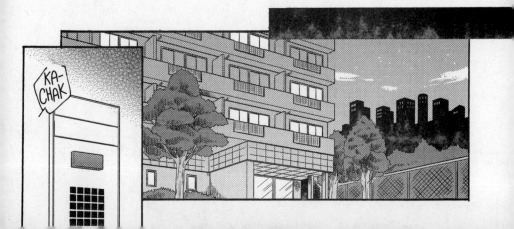

KA-CHAK

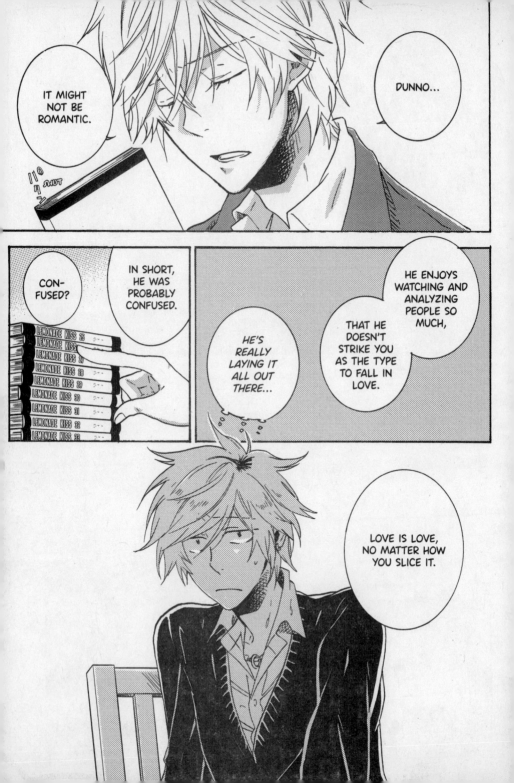

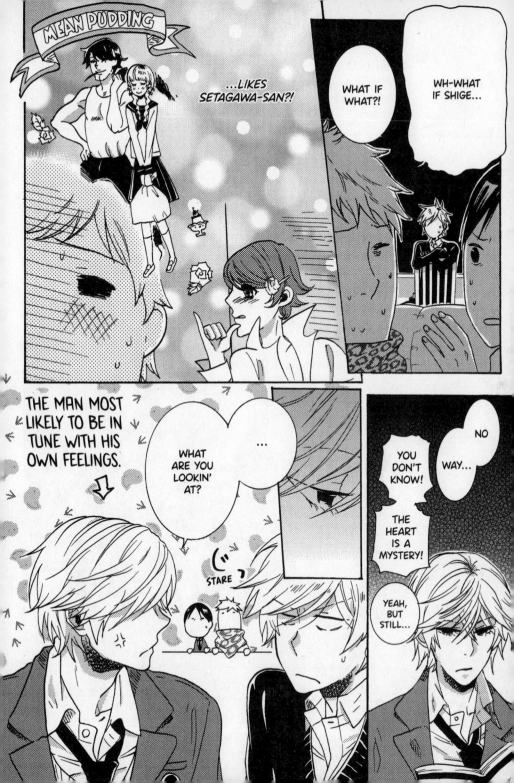

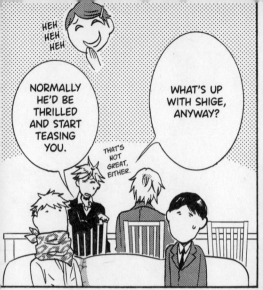

HEH HEH HEH

NORMALLY HE'D BE THRILLED AND START TEASING YOU.

WHAT'S UP WITH SHIGE, ANYWAY?

THAT'S NOT GREAT, EITHER.

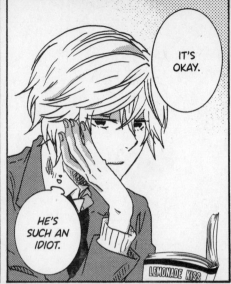

IT'S OKAY.

HE'S SUCH AN IDIOT.

LEMONADE KISS

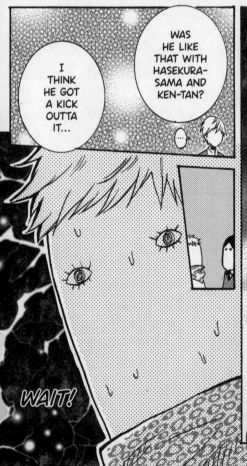

WAS HE LIKE THAT WITH HASEKURA-SAMA AND KEN-TAN?

I THINK HE GOT A KICK OUTTA IT...

...

WAIT!

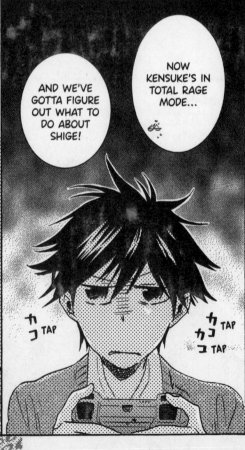

AND WE'VE GOTTA FIGURE OUT WHAT TO DO ABOUT SHIGE!

NOW KENSUKE'S IN TOTAL RAGE MODE...

カコ TAP

カコ TAP
カコ TAP

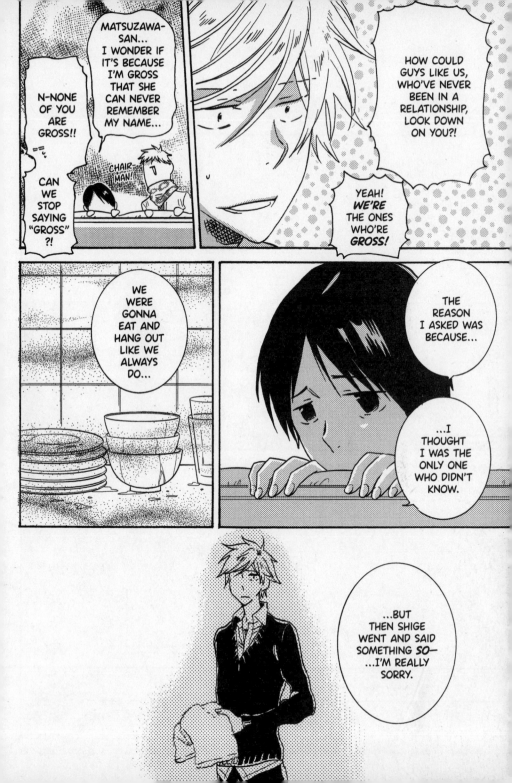

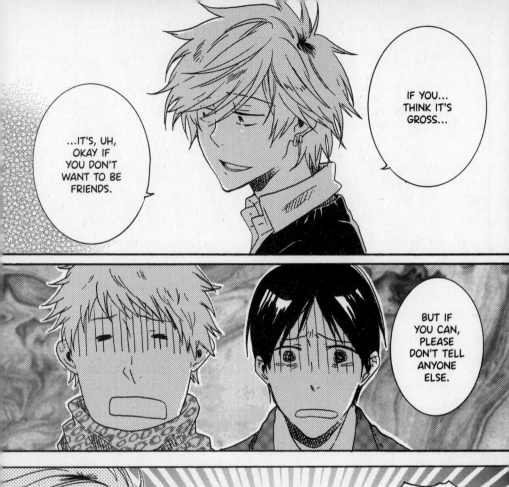

IF YOU... THINK IT'S GROSS...

...IT'S, UH, OKAY IF YOU DON'T WANT TO BE FRIENDS.

BUT IF YOU CAN, PLEASE DON'T TELL ANYONE ELSE.

WHAT?! NO WAY!!

DON'T SAY THAT!!

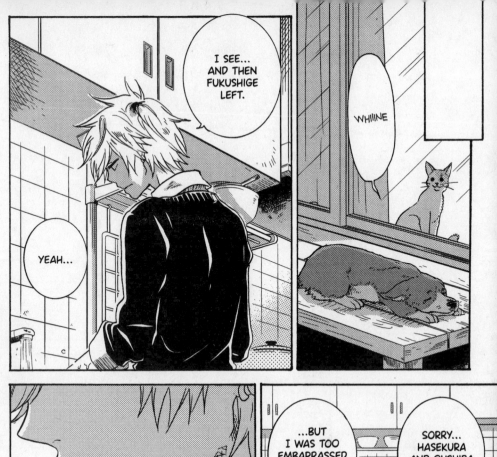

I SEE... AND THEN FUKUSHIGE LEFT.

WHIIINE

YEAH...

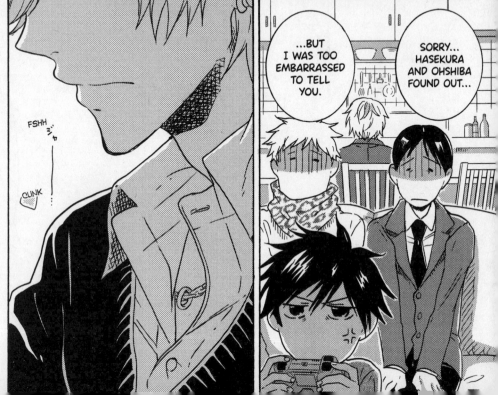

FSHH

CLINK

...BUT I WAS TOO EMBARRASSED TO TELL YOU.

SORRY... HASEKURA AND OHSHIBA FOUND OUT...

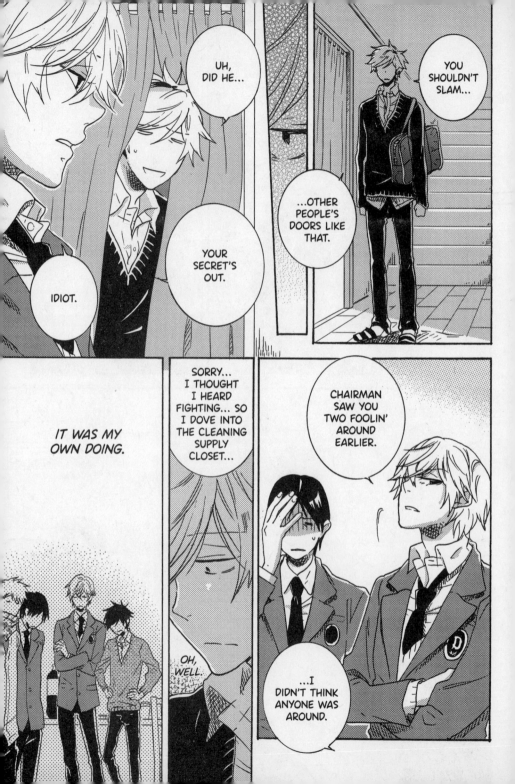

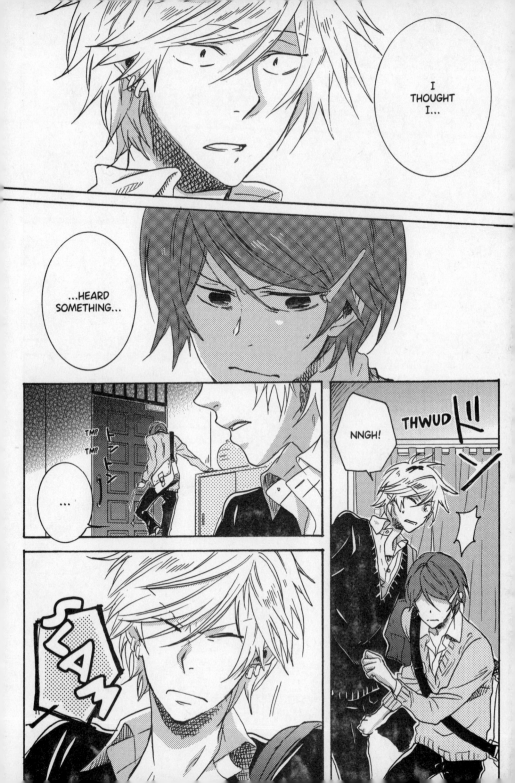

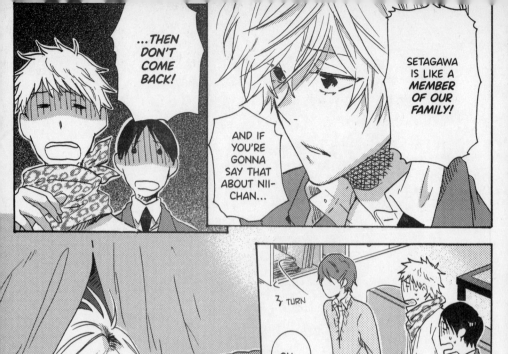

...THEN DON'T COME BACK!

SETAGAWA IS LIKE A MEMBER OF OUR FAMILY!

AND IF YOU'RE GONNA SAY THAT ABOUT NII-CHAN...

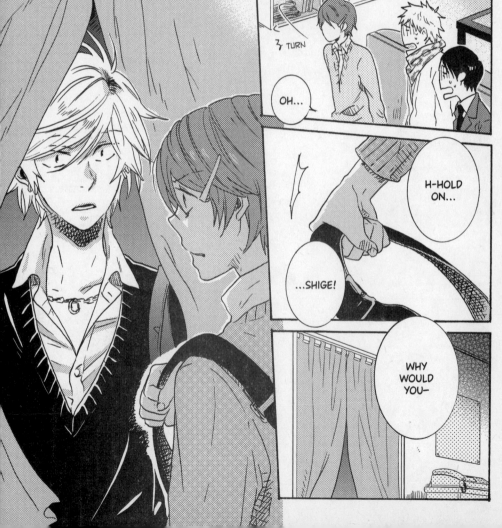

TURN

OH...

H-HOLD ON...

...SHIGE!

WHY WOULD YOU–

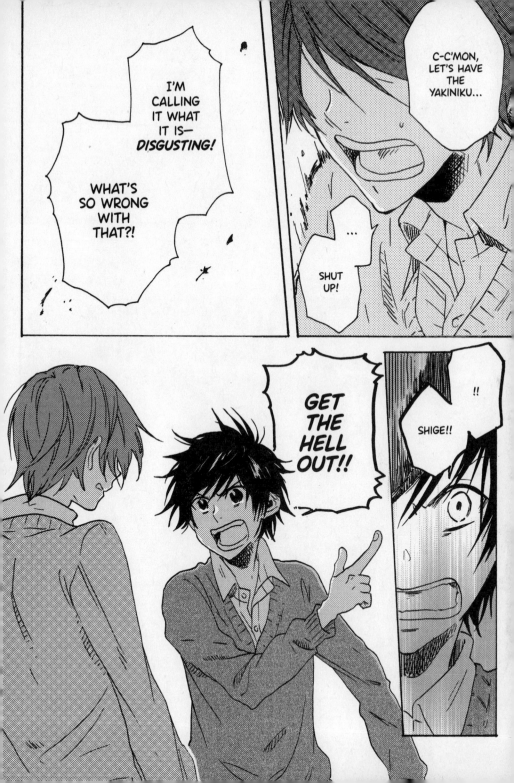

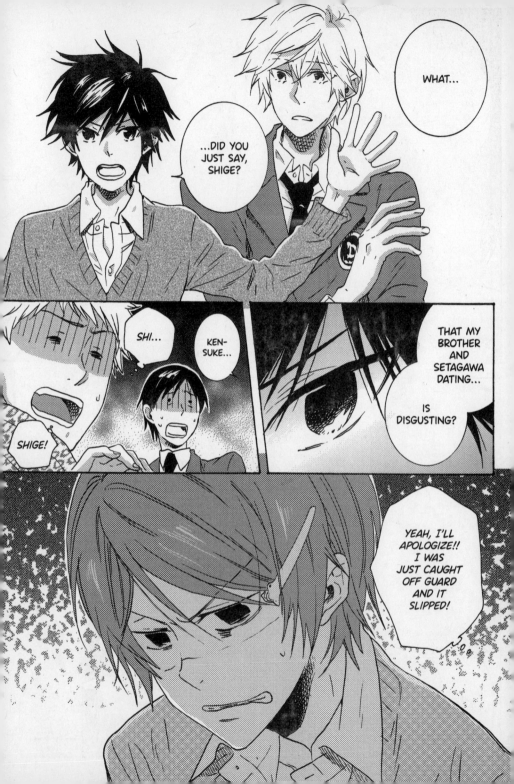

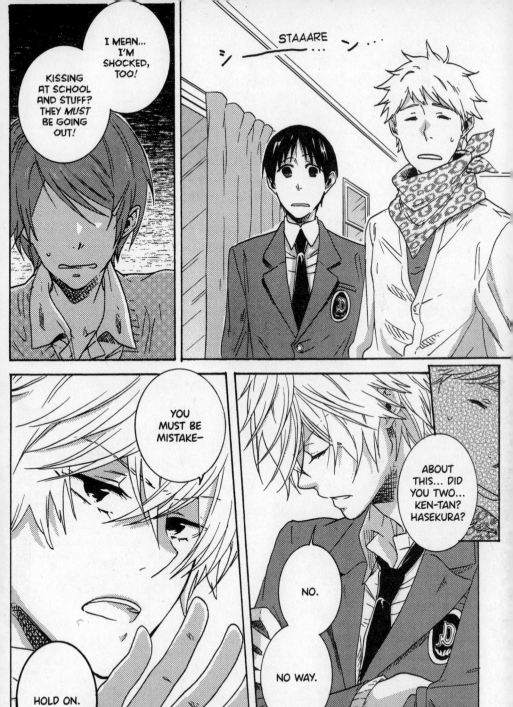

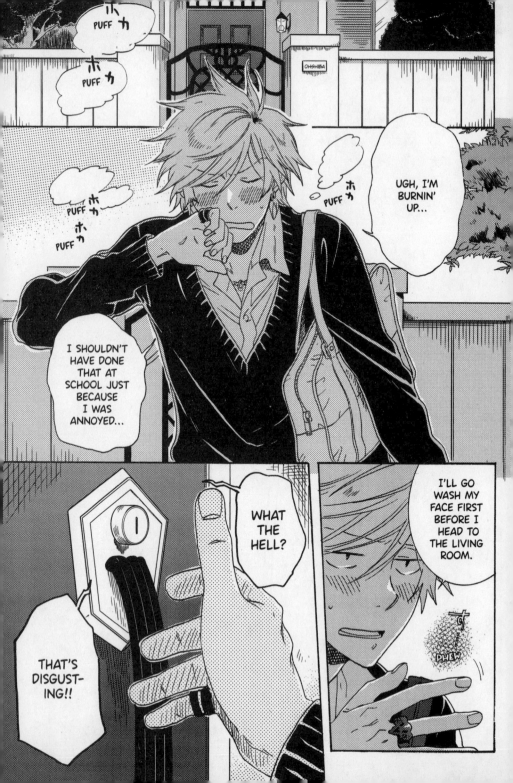

...along an
embank-
ment.

Walks
are
best...

- Shigeo

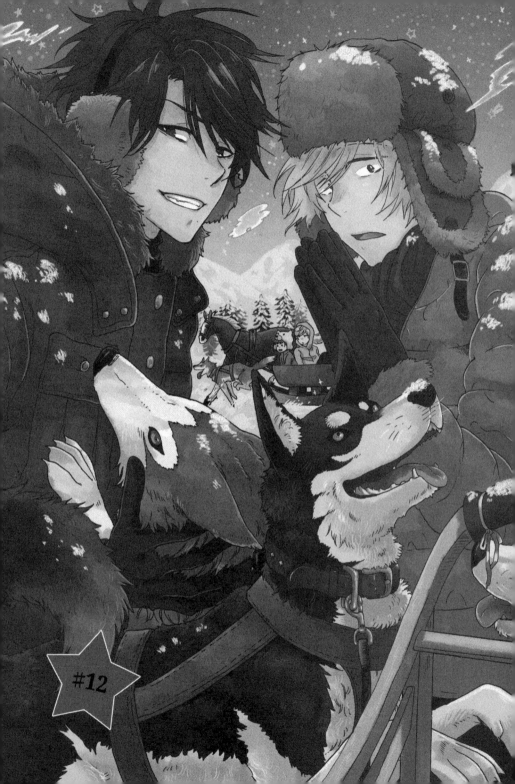

#12

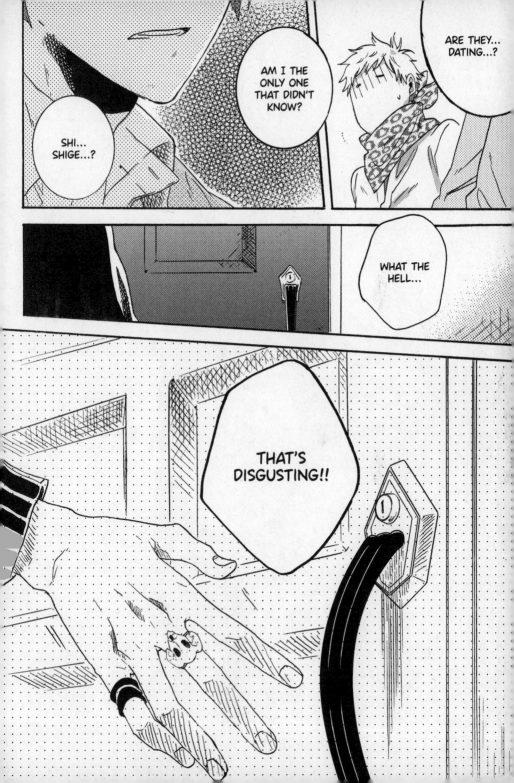

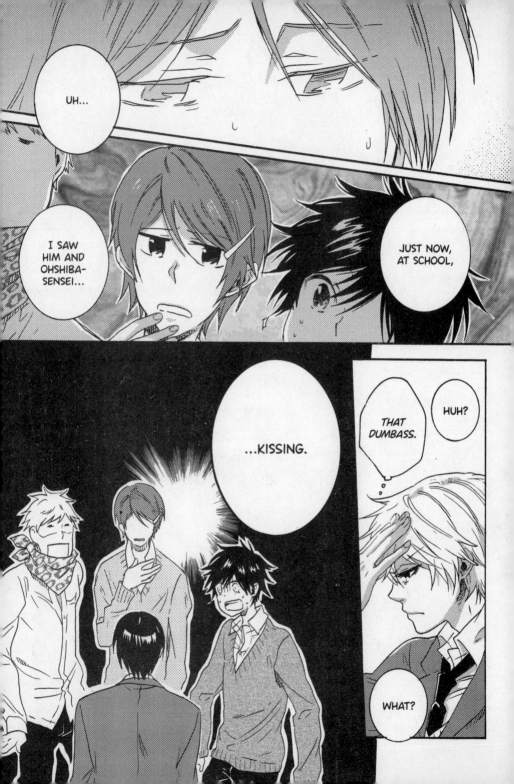

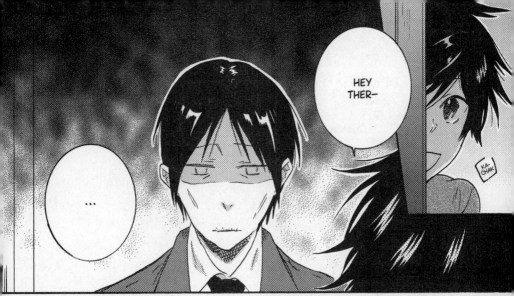

HEY THER–

...

KA-CHAK

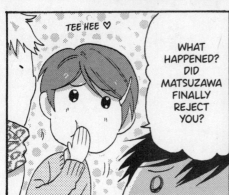

TEE HEE ♡

WHAT HAPPENED? DID MATSUZAWA FINALLY REJECT YOU?

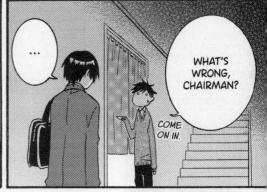

...

WHAT'S WRONG, CHAIRMAN?

COME ON IN.

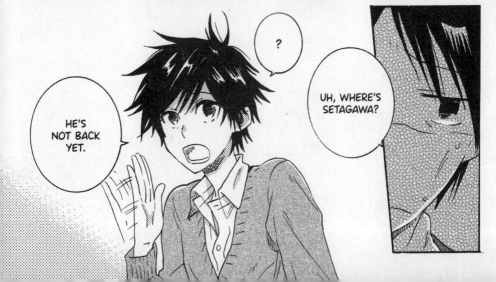

?

UH, WHERE'S SETAGAWA?

HE'S NOT BACK YET.

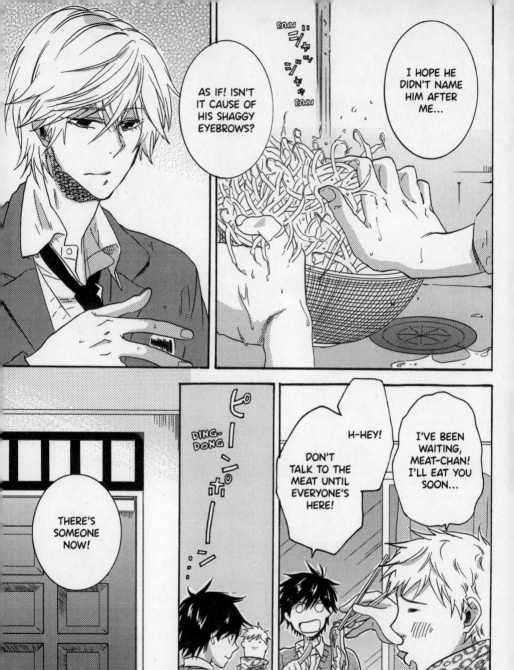

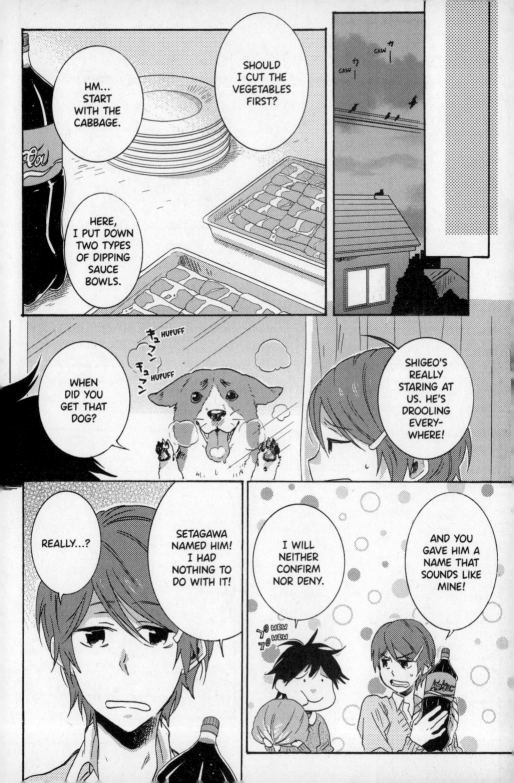

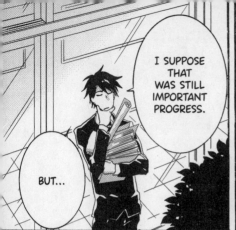

I SUPPOSE THAT WAS STILL IMPORTANT PROGRESS.

BUT...

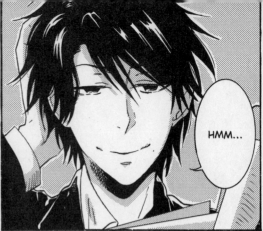

HMM...

CREAK!

HE...

...WHAT AM I GONNA— HMM, WOULD THAT BE TOO MUCH?

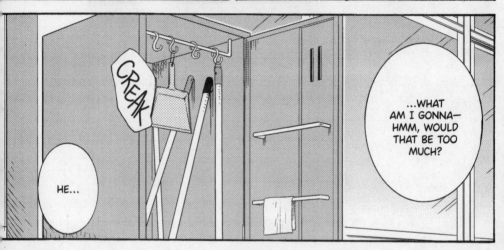

...DEFINITELY BIT MY BOTTOM LIP.

AND LEFT WITHOUT FINISHING THE SEXY STUFF *HE* STARTED.

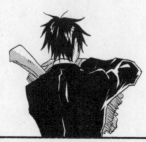

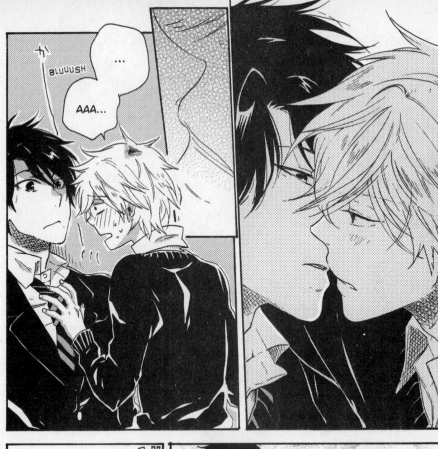

...

BLUUUSH

AAA...

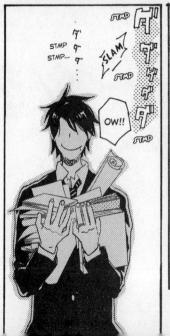

STMP
STMP...

STMP

SLAM

STMP

STMP

OW!!

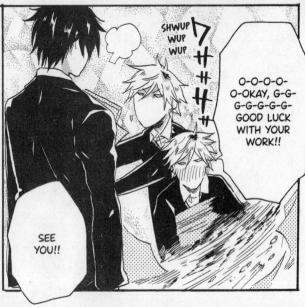

SHWUP
WUP
WUP

O-O-O-O-O-OKAY, G-G-G-G-G-G-GOOD LUCK WITH YOUR WORK!!

SEE YOU!!

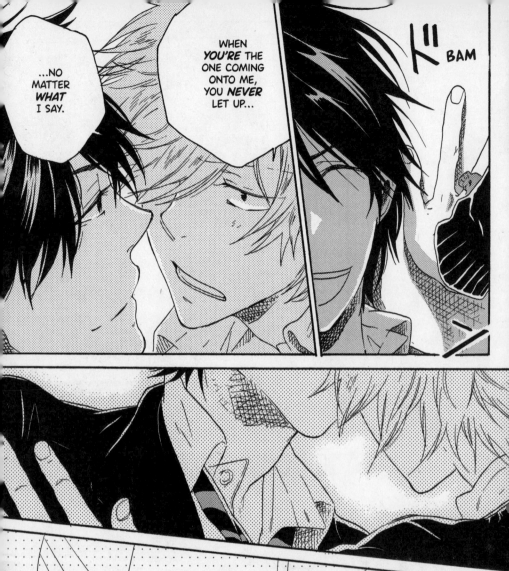

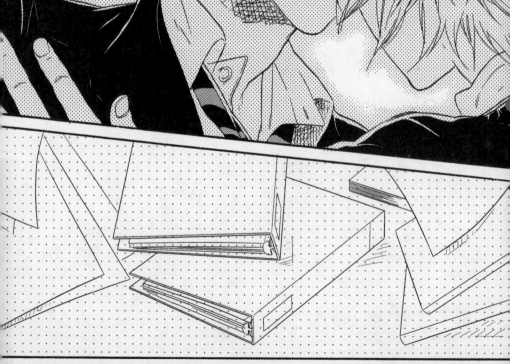

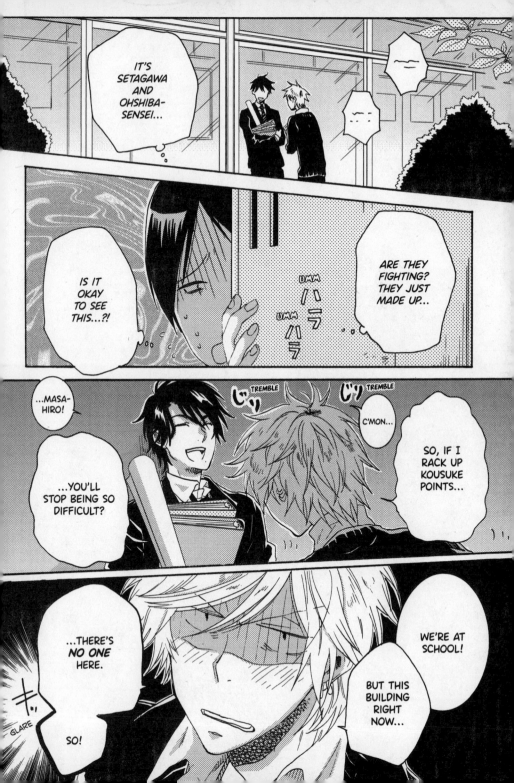

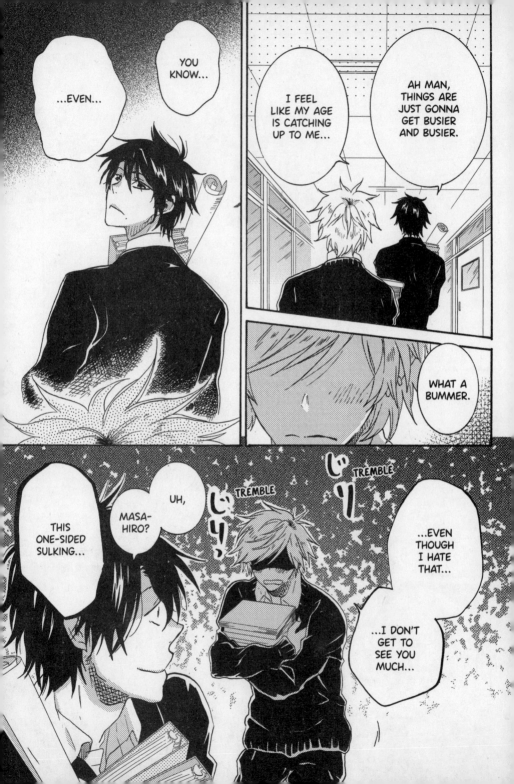

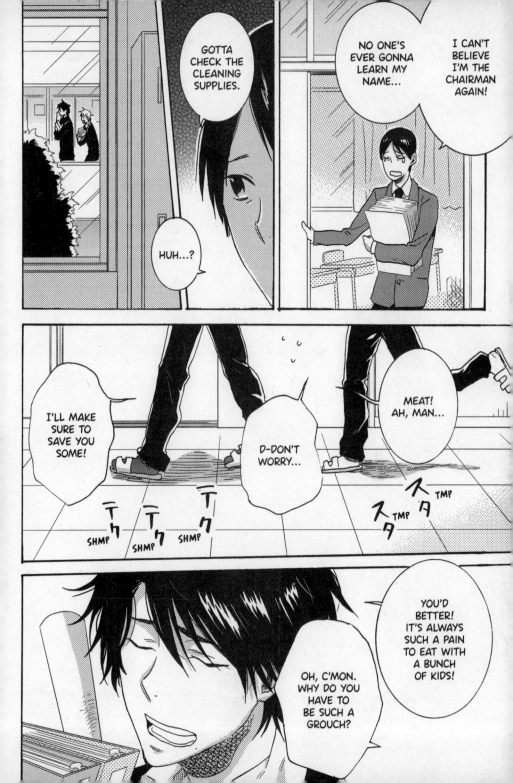

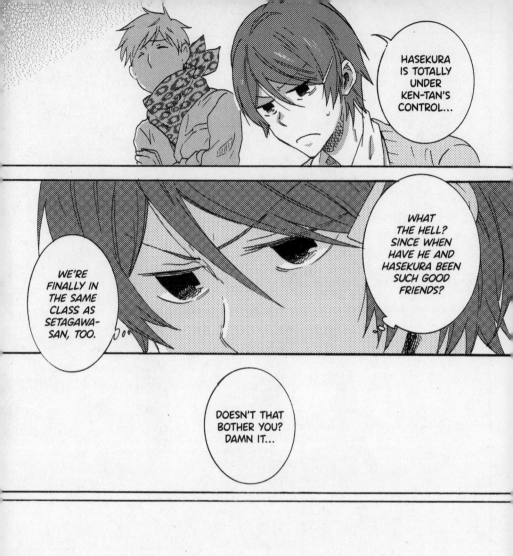

HASEKURA IS TOTALLY UNDER KEN-TAN'S CONTROL...

WHAT THE HELL? SINCE WHEN HAVE HE AND HASEKURA BEEN SUCH GOOD FRIENDS?

WE'RE FINALLY IN THE SAME CLASS AS SETAGAWA-SAN, TOO.

DOESN'T THAT BOTHER YOU? DAMN IT...

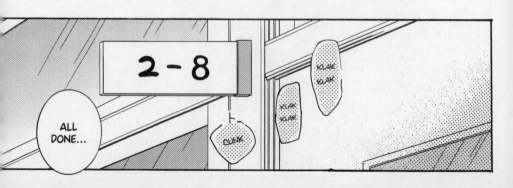

2-8

KLAK KLAK

KLAK KLAK

CLINK

ALL DONE...

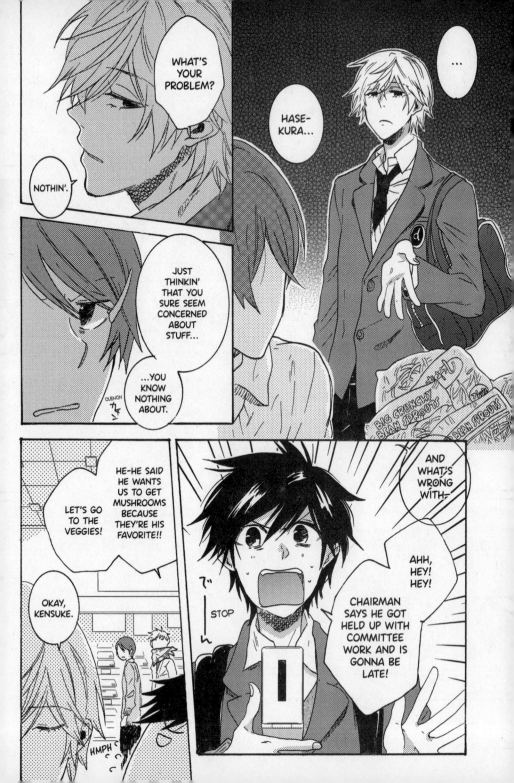

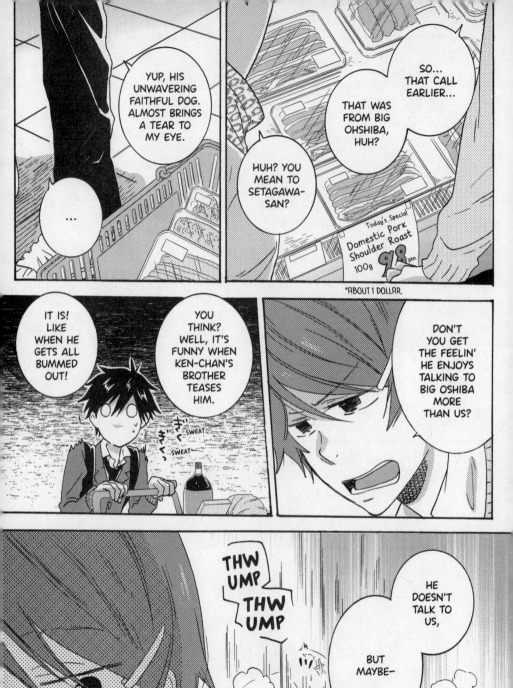

YUP, HIS UNWAVERING FAITHFUL DOG. ALMOST BRINGS A TEAR TO MY EYE.

...

SO... THAT CALL EARLIER...

THAT WAS FROM BIG OHSHIBA, HUH?

HUH? YOU MEAN TO SETAGAWA-SAN?

Today's Special
Domestic Pork Shoulder Roast
100g 98 yen

*ABOUT 1 DOLLAR.

IT IS! LIKE WHEN HE GETS ALL BUMMED OUT!

YOU THINK? WELL, IT'S FUNNY WHEN KEN-CHAN'S BROTHER TEASES HIM.

SWEAT
SWEAT

DON'T YOU GET THE FEELIN' HE ENJOYS TALKING TO BIG OSHIBA MORE THAN US?

THW UMP
THW UMP

HE DOESN'T TALK TO US,

BUT MAYBE—

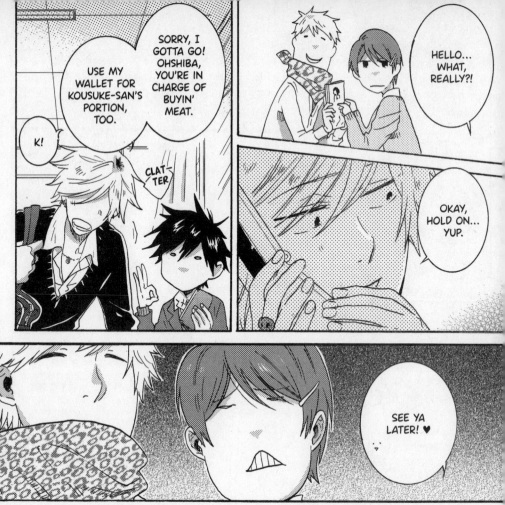

SORRY, I GOTTA GO! OHSHIBA, YOU'RE IN CHARGE OF BUYIN' MEAT.

USE MY WALLET FOR KOUSUKE-SAN'S PORTION, TOO.

K!

CLAT-TER

HELLO... WHAT, REALLY?!

OKAY, HOLD ON... YUP.

SEE YA LATER! ❤

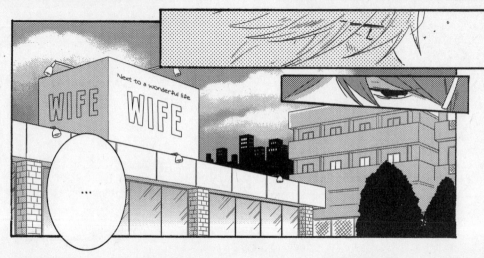

WIFE

WIFE

Next to a wonderful life

...

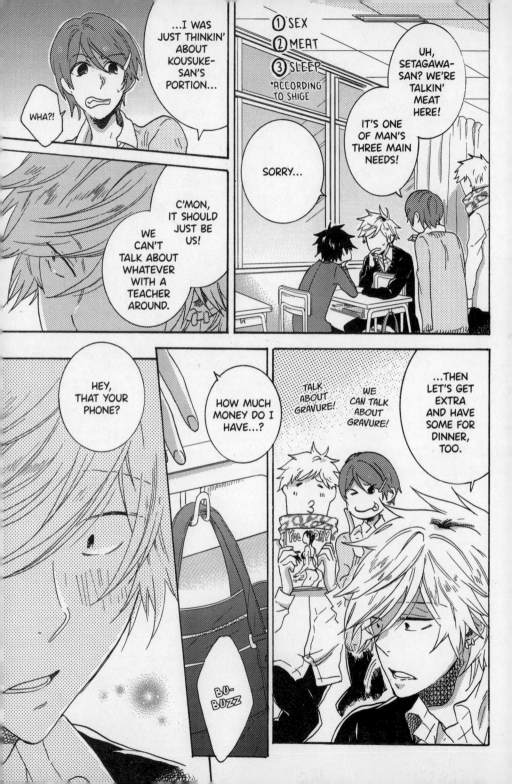

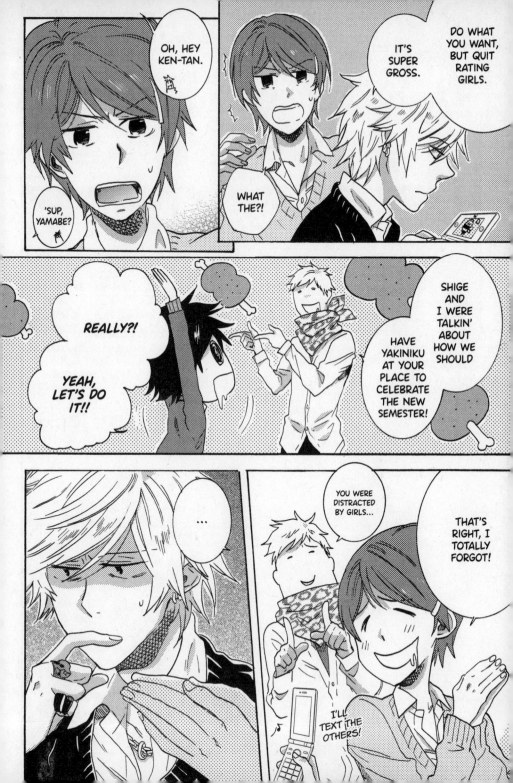

BA-DUMP BA-DUMP

WHAT TO EAT, HUH...?

HA HA

O-OH, JUST WONDERIN' WHAT TO EAT TODAY...

HM? DID I INTERRUPT SOMETHING?

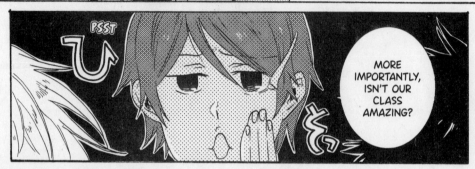

PSST

MORE IMPORTANTLY, ISN'T OUR CLASS AMAZING?

SSF

OH, COOL...

I DID A LAP OF THE BUILDING, AND EVEN THE FIRST YEARS ARE CUTE!

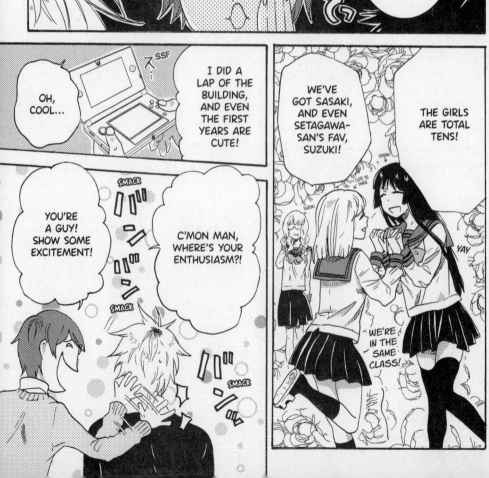

WE'VE GOT SASAKI, AND EVEN SETAGAWA-SAN'S FAV, SUZUKI!

THE GIRLS ARE TOTAL TENS!

YOU'RE A GUY! SHOW SOME EXCITEMENT!

SMACK

C'MON MAN, WHERE'S YOUR ENTHUSIASM?!

SMACK

SMACK

WE'RE IN THE SAME CLASS!

YAY

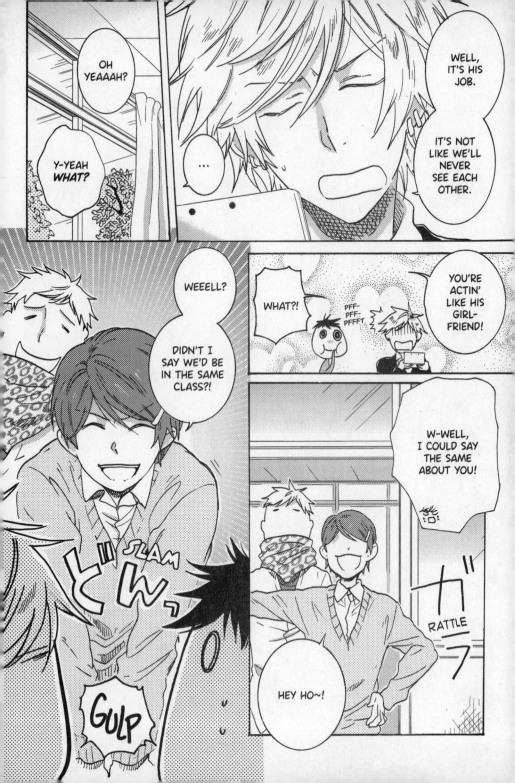

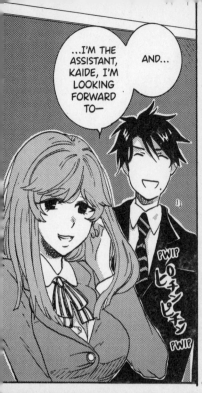

...I'M THE ASSISTANT, KAIDE, I'M LOOKING FORWARD TO—

AND...

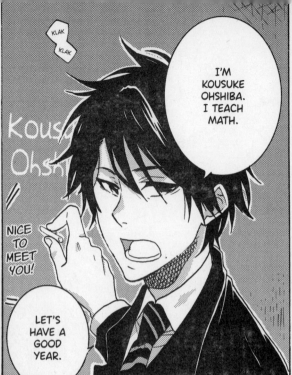

KLAK
KLAK

Kousu
Ohsh

I'M KOUSUKE OHSHIBA. I TEACH MATH.

NICE TO MEET YOU!

PWIP
PWIP

LET'S HAVE A GOOD YEAR.

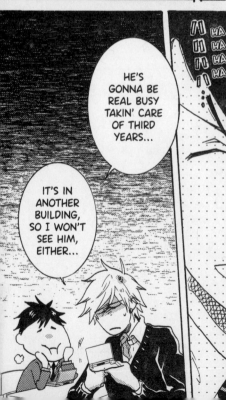

HE'S GONNA BE REAL BUSY TAKIN' CARE OF THIRD YEARS...

HA HA HA HA HA

IT'S IN ANOTHER BUILDING, SO I WON'T SEE HIM, EITHER...

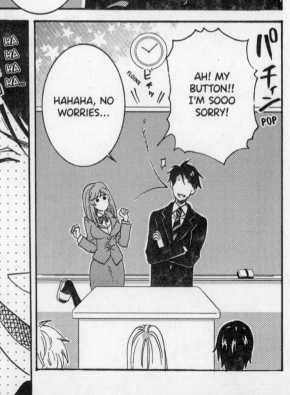

HAHAHA, NO WORRIES...

FLOINK

AH! MY BUTTON!! I'M SOOO SORRY!

POP

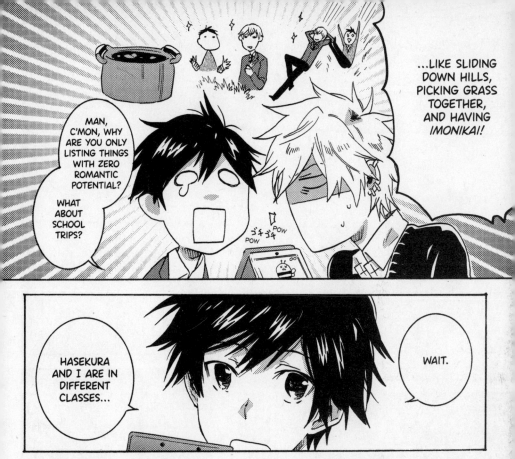

...LIKE SLIDING DOWN HILLS, PICKING GRASS TOGETHER, AND HAVING IMONIKAI!

MAN, C'MON, WHY ARE YOU ONLY LISTING THINGS WITH ZERO ROMANTIC POTENTIAL?

WHAT ABOUT SCHOOL TRIPS?

HASEKURA AND I ARE IN DIFFERENT CLASSES...

WAIT.

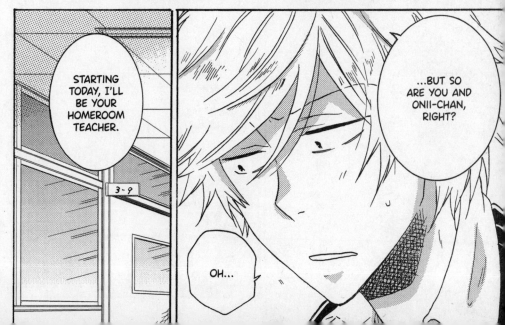

STARTING TODAY, I'LL BE YOUR HOMEROOM TEACHER.

3-9

...BUT SO ARE YOU AND ONII-CHAN, RIGHT?

OH...

GAAAPE

...OHSHIBA?

2 - 3

CONGRATS ON BARELY PASSING...

...OHSHIBA-KUN!

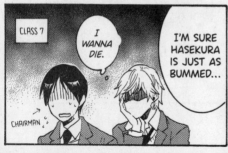

CLASS 7

I WANNA DIE.

I'M SURE HASEKURA IS JUST AS BUMMED...

CHAIRMAN

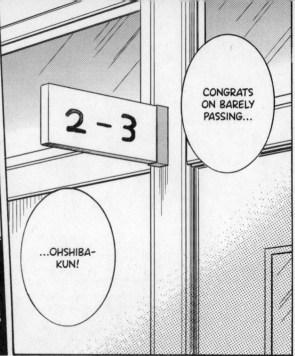

AUGH

D-DON'T FORGET THE CHAIRMAN!

IT'S NOT YOUR FAULT. IT'S GOT NOTHING TO DO WITH OUR GRADES.

THIS IS NO TIME TO CELEBRATE! HASEKURA AND I ARE IN DIFFERENT CLASSES!!

WHOA

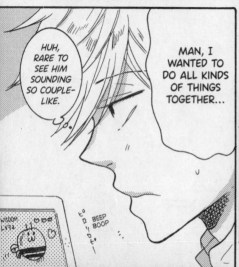

HUH, RARE TO SEE HIM SOUNDING SO COUPLE-LIKE.

MAN, I WANTED TO DO ALL KINDS OF THINGS TOGETHER...

WISDOM LV92

BEEP BOOP

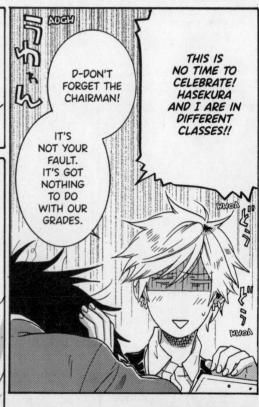

WHOA

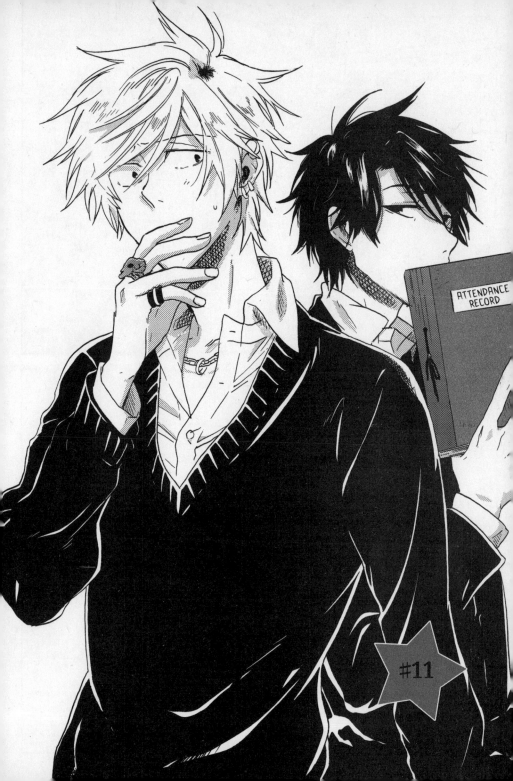

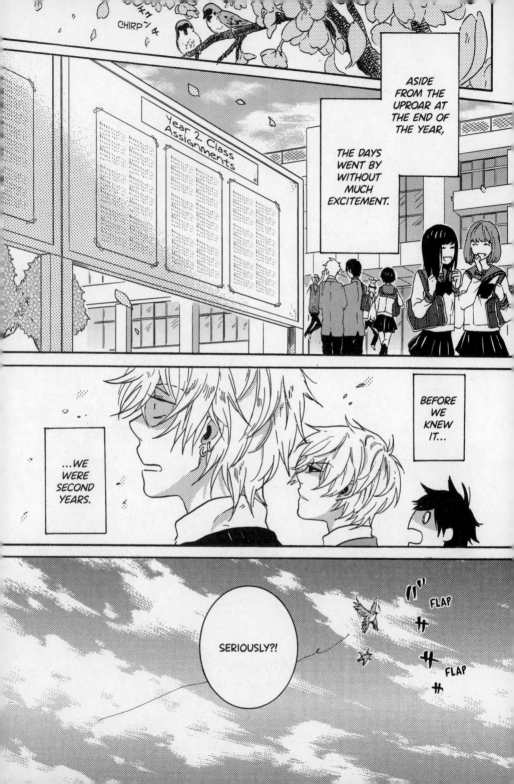

CHIRP

Year 2 Class Assignments

ASIDE FROM THE UPROAR AT THE END OF THE YEAR,

THE DAYS WENT BY WITHOUT MUCH EXCITEMENT.

BEFORE WE KNEW IT...

...WE WERE SECOND YEARS.

SERIOUSLY?!

FLAP

FLAP

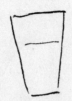

HARD WATER   SOFT WATER

Supposedly it's better to
cook rice and boil pasta in
hard water (makes sense).

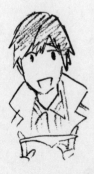

Q: Why do you wear panties on your head?

A: At first, I was just goofin' around, but then people were so offended by it, so it kinda became thrilling! What can you do?!

HARD OR SOFT?

NATSUO! WATER!

EITHER!

LOOK! YOU MADE MASAHIRO FAINT!

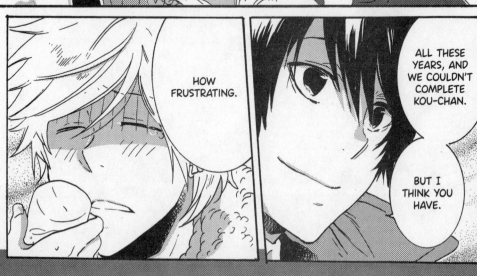

HOW FRUSTRATING.

ALL THESE YEARS, AND WE COULDN'T COMPLETE KOU-CHAN.

BUT I THINK YOU HAVE.

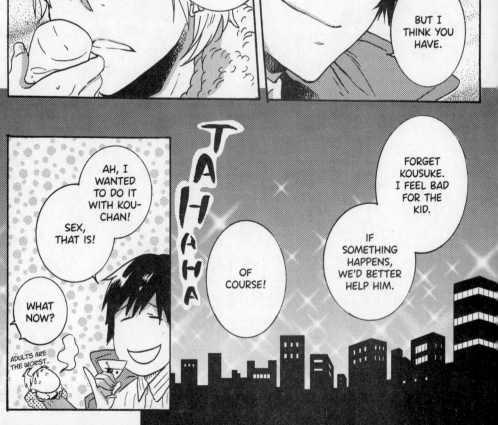

AH, I WANTED TO DO IT WITH KOU-CHAN!

SEX, THAT IS!

WHAT NOW?

TAHAHA

OF COURSE!

FORGET KOUSUKE. I FEEL BAD FOR THE KID.

IF SOMETHING HAPPENS, WE'D BETTER HELP HIM.

ADULTS ARE THE WORST—

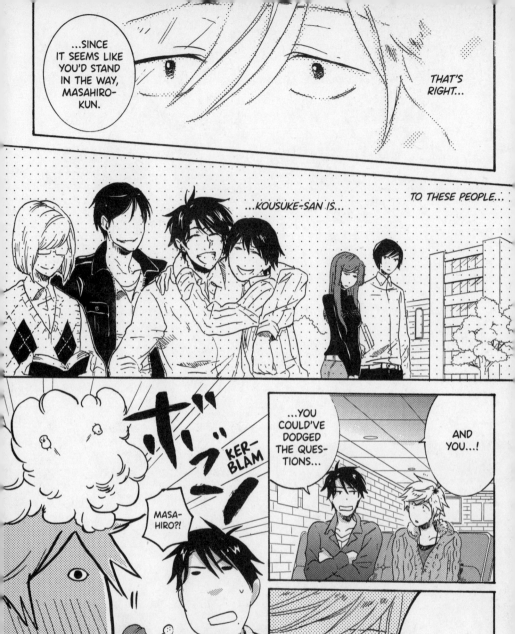

...SINCE IT SEEMS LIKE YOU'D STAND IN THE WAY, MASAHIRO-KUN.

THAT'S RIGHT...

...KOUSUKE-SAN IS...

TO, THESE PEOPLE...

KER-BLAM

MASA-HIRO?!

...YOU COULD'VE DODGED THE QUESTIONS...

AND YOU...!

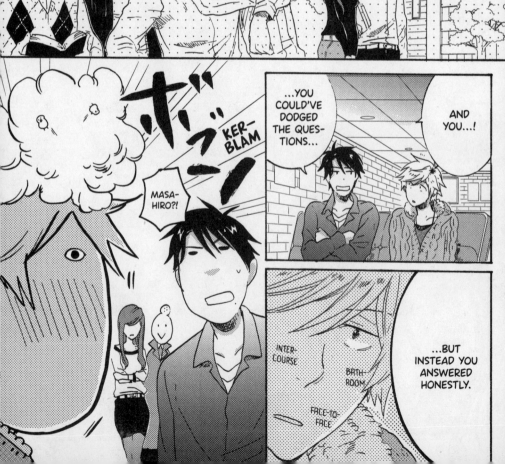

INTER-COURSE

BATH-ROOM

FACE-TO-FACE

...BUT INSTEAD YOU ANSWERED HONESTLY.

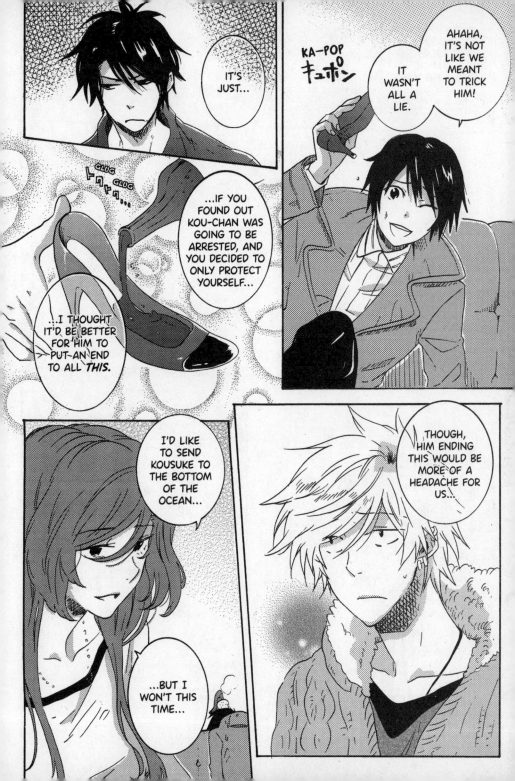

MORE LIKE PERV MODE!

I WENT INTO WORK MODE...

UH...

WAIT...

HAHA, MY BAD...

WHEN DID I TELL YOU TO GO THAT FAR?

JEEZ...

YOU'VE GOT NO RIGHT TO TEST MASAHIRO LIKE THAT.

WAS THAT ALL A LIE?!

ぽい
DROP

SHE'S GOT SOME BURNING DESIRE TO SEE HIM FACE-TO-FACE.

...

BUT I'M STILL RILED UP.

TWO OF KOUSUKE-SAN'S FRIENDS...

FINE...

NEXT WEEK, THEN.

HEY, THERE!

SORRY FOR THE SUDDEN INVITE!

IT WAS URGENT.

...WANNA SEE ME?

HUH? IS KOU-CHAN NOT BACK YET?

NOPE!

I WONDER IF...

...I'LL EVER GET USED TO ALL THIS...

ギクッ GULP

U-UH, MAYBE?

GUESS HE'S STAYING OVER TONIGHT.

YAWN~

DID HE GET A GIRLFRIEND AGAIN? DO YOU KNOW?

I SAW HIM WEARING A RING!

O-OH YEAH?

Katsudon

#2.5 was Houjou's first appearance
(Sometime during first year when Kousuke
and Setagawa weren't dating yet.)

← Spring of year two starts
from the next page!

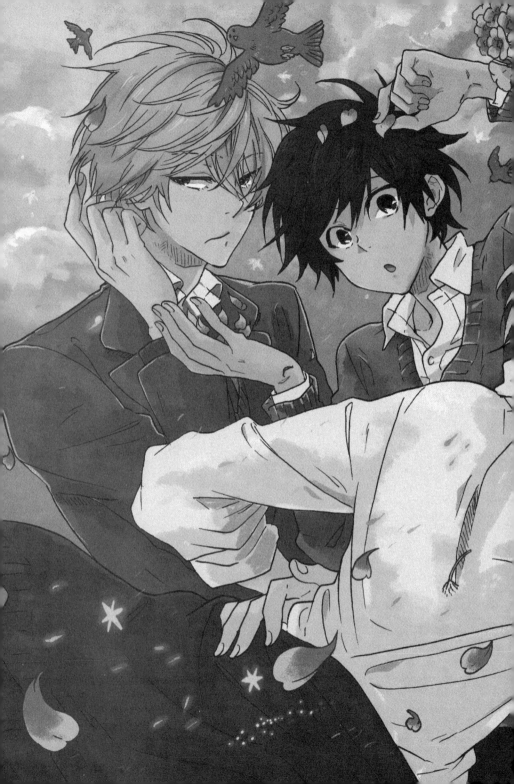

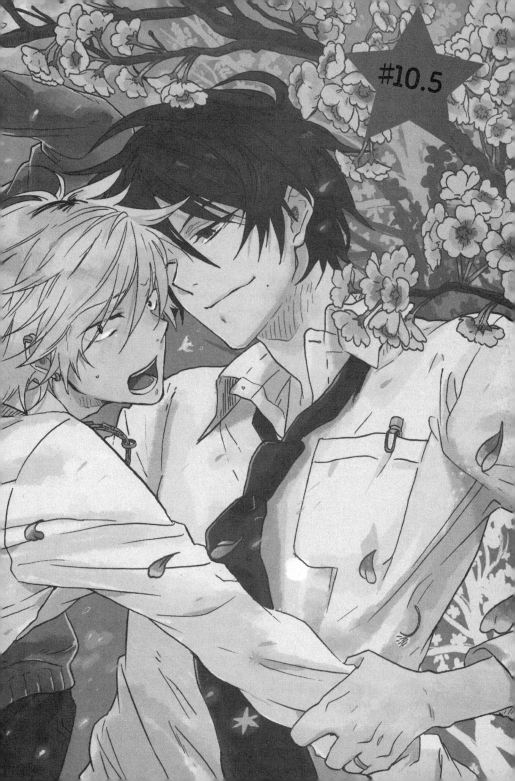

#10.5

DAZZLING MEMECO-STYLE WONDERLAND OPEN ☆

BAD ADULTS WILL
BE PUNISHED!

THE ADULTS

KNOW EVERYTHING IN AN INSTANT!! HITORIJIME SERIES
RELATIONSHIP CHART

TSUNEHITO
HOUJOU

DETECTIVE
WHO LOVES
PANTIES

SHIGEO

WOOF

FOUR-
LEGGED
FRIENDS

MARRIED

AYAKA
HOUJOU

SURROUNDED BY
WEIRD MEN

MATH TEACHER

KOUSUKE
OHSHIBA

MEOW

SASANISHIKI

BROTHERS

NATSUO

KENSUKE
OHSHIBA

LOVES
KARAOKE

MOM

BARTENDER,
LIKES TROPICAL
FISH

ALWAYS
FULL OF
ENERGY

LITTLE BROTHER

ASAYA
HASEKURA

EATS BIG
MEALS

OHSHIBA
FAMILY

MY FOOD
ISN'T BAD!

ITALIAN-TYPE,
STILL AN
UNKNOWN

YUGE

THE MAIN FOUR CHARACTERS OF THE HITORIJIME SERIES.
IT ALL SEEMS TO REVOLVE AROUND THE OHSHIBA FAMILY?
FULL-ON FEELINGS UNDER ONE ROOF.

CLASSMATES

FUKUSHIGE

CHAIRMAN

TRENDSTER

POSSIBLE
LESBIAN

RYOUKO

LOVE TO
TEASE PEOPLE

YAMABE

SERIOUS

MATSUZAWA

SMALL

SATOU

DYING THE CHICK
PUDDING BLACK!

CUTE CAN BE MADE
(CONFIRMED)

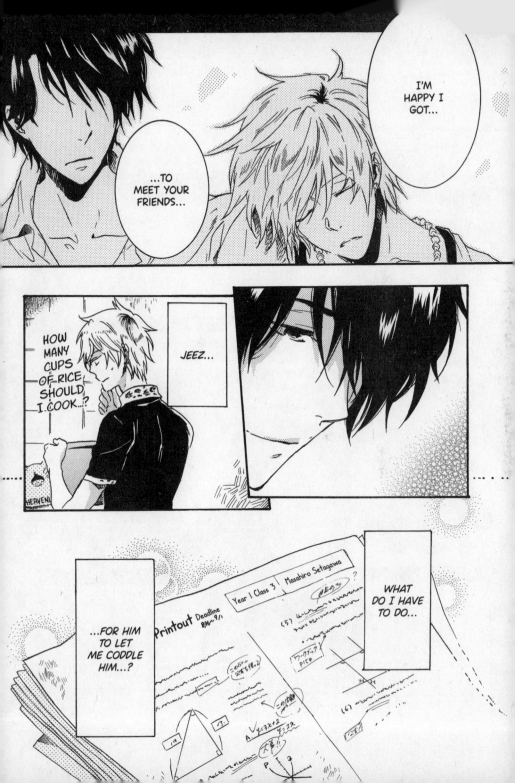

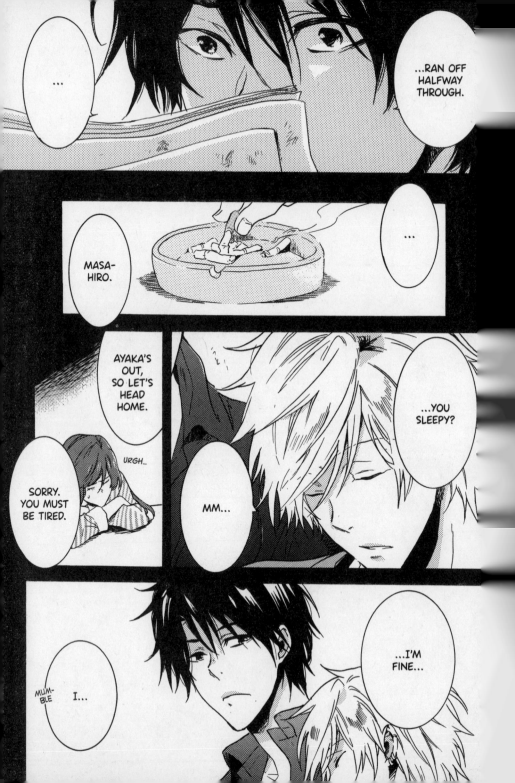

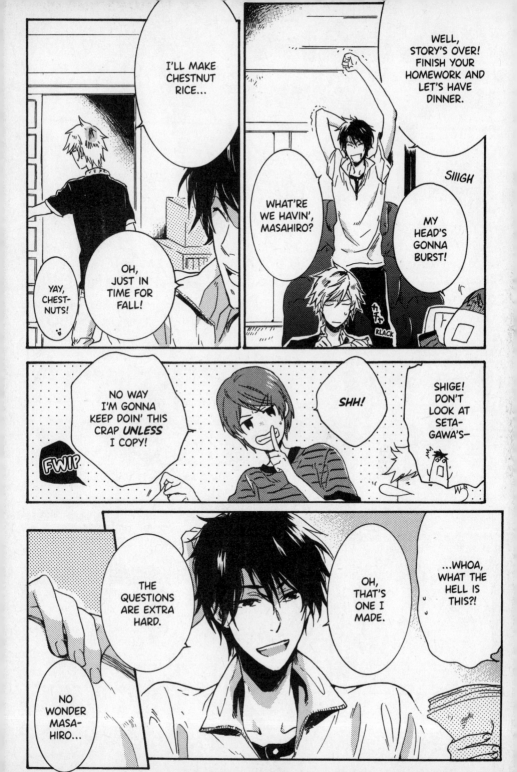

AFTER THAT...

"I PRAY I DON'T SEE YOU IN JUVIE...!"

...WE LISTENED TO AYAKA COMPLAIN UNTIL MORNING.

ぱたん
THWUMP

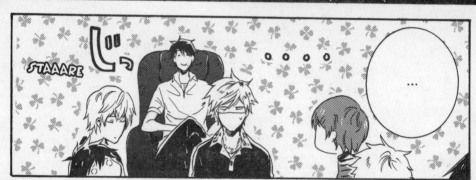

STAAARE

...

AHAHA! I'LL KEEP THAT IN MIND.

...I GUESS SOME PEOPLE REALLY LIVE LIKE THAT.

I HATE THAT *THAT'S* A MEMBER OF MY FAMILY...

SETAGAWA-KUN, THINGS END POORLY FOR YOU NO MATTER WHO YOU MEET, HUH...

POOR THING, SURROUNDED BY WEIRDOS.

UH, WELL...

ゴーヤ

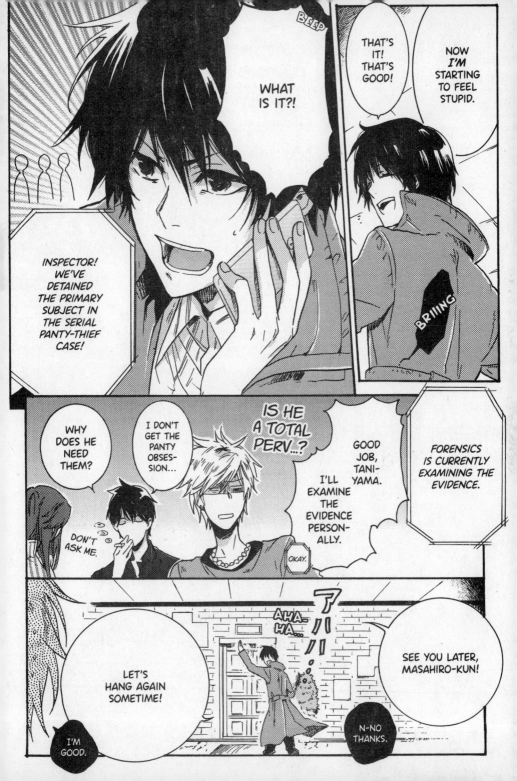

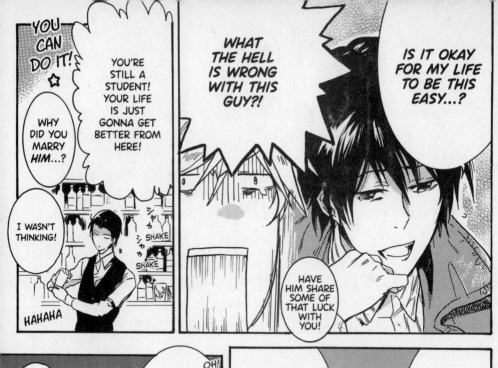

YOU CAN DO IT! ☆

WHY DID YOU MARRY HIM...?

I WASN'T THINKING!

YOU'RE STILL A STUDENT! YOUR LIFE IS JUST GONNA GET BETTER FROM HERE!

SHAKE SHAKE SHAKE

HAHAHA

WHAT THE HELL IS WRONG WITH THIS GUY?!

IS IT OKAY FOR MY LIFE TO BE THIS EASY...?

HAVE HIM SHARE SOME OF THAT LUCK WITH YOU!

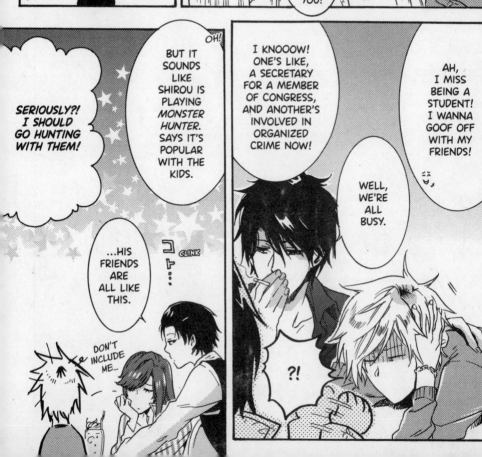

SERIOUSLY?! I SHOULD GO HUNTING WITH THEM!

OH!

BUT IT SOUNDS LIKE SHIROU IS PLAYING MONSTER HUNTER. SAYS IT'S POPULAR WITH THE KIDS.

...HIS FRIENDS ARE ALL LIKE THIS.

CLINK

DON'T INCLUDE ME...

I KNOOOW! ONE'S LIKE, A SECRETARY FOR A MEMBER OF CONGRESS, AND ANOTHER'S INVOLVED IN ORGANIZED CRIME NOW!

AH, I MISS BEING A STUDENT! I WANNA GOOF OFF WITH MY FRIENDS!

WELL, WE'RE ALL BUSY.

?!

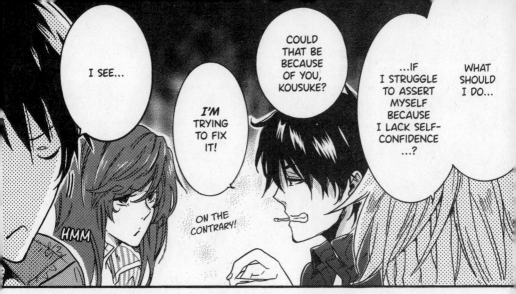

I SEE...

I'M TRYING TO FIX IT!

COULD THAT BE BECAUSE OF YOU, KOUSUKE?

...IF I STRUGGLE TO ASSERT MYSELF BECAUSE I LACK SELF-CONFIDENCE...?

WHAT SHOULD I DO...

HMM

ON THE CONTRARY!

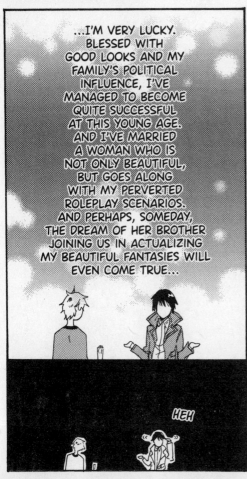

...I'M VERY LUCKY. BLESSED WITH GOOD LOOKS AND MY FAMILY'S POLITICAL INFLUENCE, I'VE MANAGED TO BECOME QUITE SUCCESSFUL AT THIS YOUNG AGE. AND I'VE MARRIED A WOMAN WHO IS NOT ONLY BEAUTIFUL, BUT GOES ALONG WITH MY PERVERTED ROLEPLAY SCENARIOS. AND PERHAPS, SOMEDAY, THE DREAM OF HER BROTHER JOINING US IN ACTUALIZING MY BEAUTIFUL FANTASIES WILL EVEN COME TRUE...

HEH

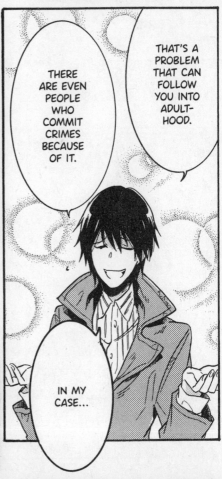

THERE ARE EVEN PEOPLE WHO COMMIT CRIMES BECAUSE OF IT.

THAT'S A PROBLEM THAT CAN FOLLOW YOU INTO ADULT-HOOD.

IN MY CASE...

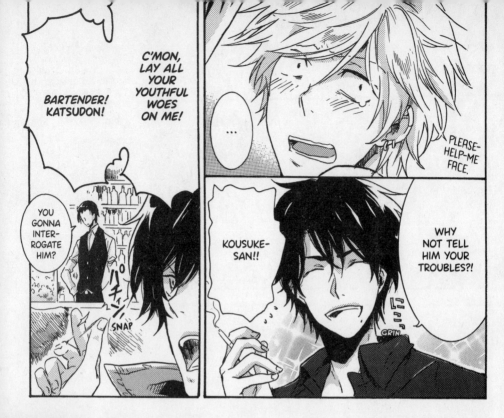
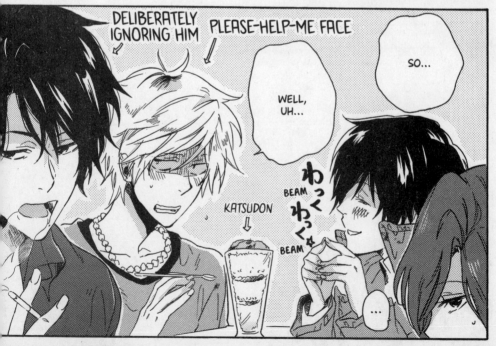

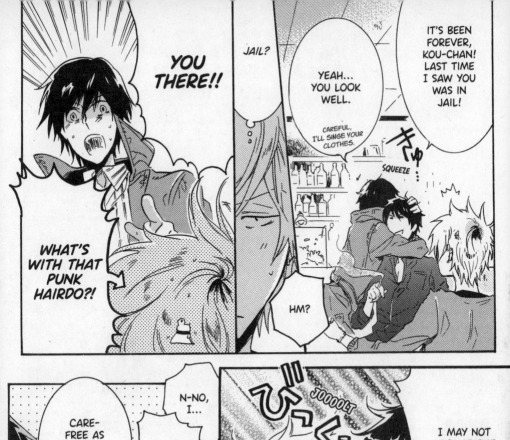

YOU THERE!!

WHAT'S WITH THAT PUNK HAIRDO?!

JAIL?

IT'S BEEN FOREVER, KOU-CHAN! LAST TIME I SAW YOU WAS IN JAIL!

YEAH... YOU LOOK WELL.

CAREFUL, I'LL SINGE YOUR CLOTHES.

SQUEEZE

HM?

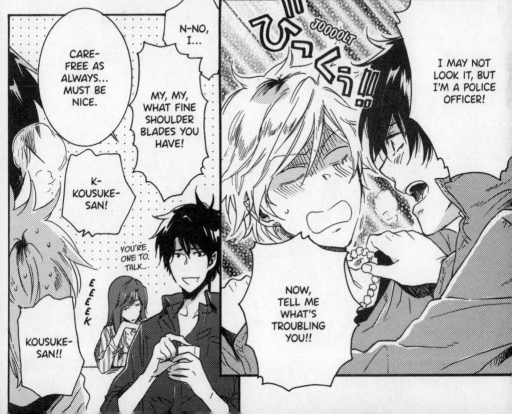

N-NO, I...

CARE-FREE AS ALWAYS... MUST BE NICE.

MY, MY, WHAT FINE SHOULDER BLADES YOU HAVE!

K-KOUSUKE-SAN!

YOU'RE ONE TO TALK...

KOUSUKE-SAN!!

EEEEK

JOOOOLT

I MAY NOT LOOK IT, BUT I'M A POLICE OFFICER!

NOW, TELL ME WHAT'S TROUBLING YOU!!

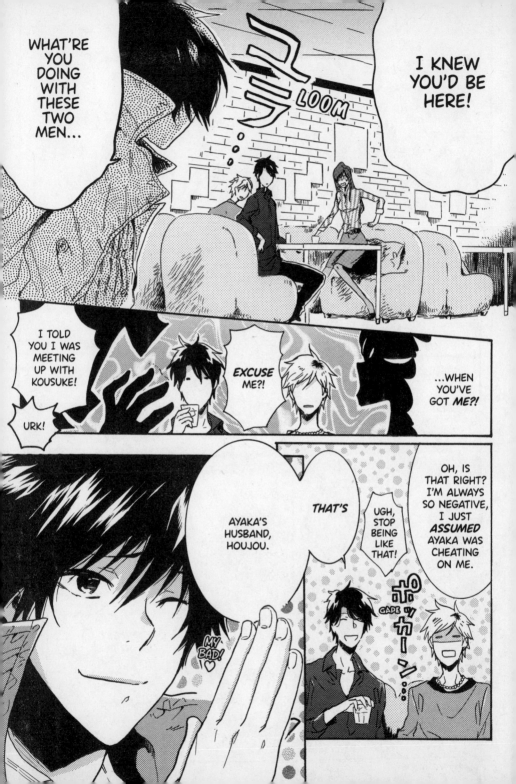

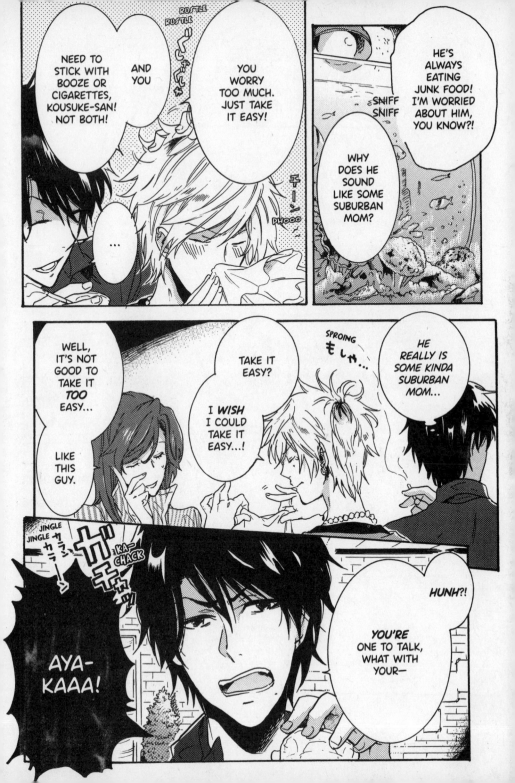

ALL RIGHT!

WHAT ABOUT YOUR HOMEWORK?!

ABSOLUTELY— ONLY BECAUSE SETAGAWA-SAN DOESN'T WANT US TO!

WANNA HEAR ABOUT IT?

H-HEY!

VWRRR

GWIM GWIM GWIM

RELAX BAR
MARY

*2ND BAR OF THE NIGHT.

LA LA LA

NO, IT'S JUST THAT I'M OVER HERE WORRYING ABOUT WHETHER HE'S EATING A BALANCED DIET...

NNGH...

SNIFF SNIFF SNIFF SNIFF SNIFF SNIFF

SORRY ABOUT MY LITTLE BROTHER.

GONNA CALL YOU "LIGHTWEIGHT."

YOU'VE BARELY HAD A DROP AND YOU'RE ALREADY PRETTY TIPSY.

OH, BOY...

...AND ALL HASEKURA DOES IS GLARE AT ME!!

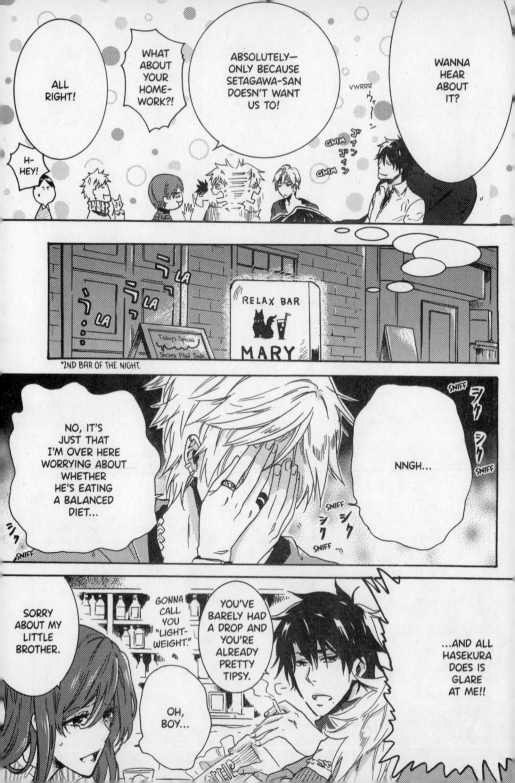

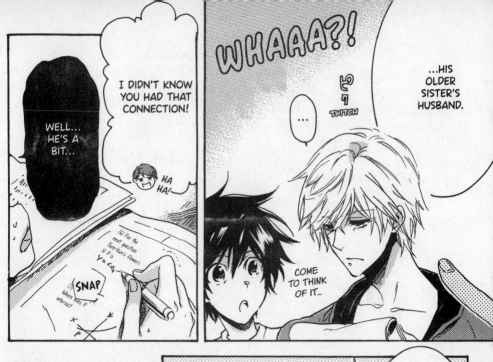

I DIDN'T KNOW YOU HAD THAT CONNECTION!

WELL... HE'S A BIT...

HA HA!

SNAP

WHAAA?!

...

TWITCH

...HIS OLDER SISTER'S HUSBAND.

COME TO THINK OF IT...

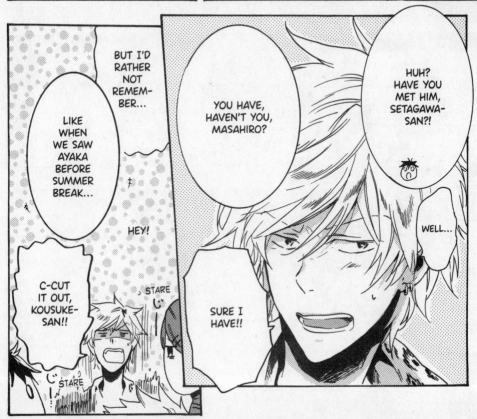

BUT I'D RATHER NOT REMEMBER...

LIKE WHEN WE SAW AYAKA BEFORE SUMMER BREAK...

HEY!

YOU HAVE, HAVEN'T YOU, MASAHIRO?

HUH? HAVE YOU MET HIM, SETAGAWA-SAN?!

WELL...

C-CUT IT OUT, KOUSUKE-SAN!!

STARE

SURE I HAVE!!

STARE

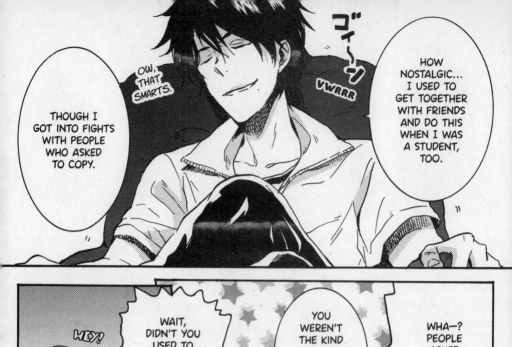

HOW NOSTALGIC... I USED TO GET TOGETHER WITH FRIENDS AND DO THIS WHEN I WAS A STUDENT, TOO.

OW, THAT SMARTS.

ゴイ〜ン VWRRR

THOUGH I GOT INTO FIGHTS WITH PEOPLE WHO ASKED TO COPY.

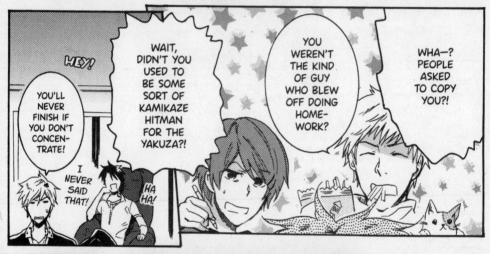

WHA—? PEOPLE ASKED TO COPY YOU?!

YOU WEREN'T THE KIND OF GUY WHO BLEW OFF DOING HOME-WORK?

WAIT, DIDN'T YOU USED TO BE SOME SORT OF KAMIKAZE HITMAN FOR THE YAKUZA?!

HEY!

YOU'LL NEVER FINISH IF YOU DON'T CONCEN-TRATE!

I NEVER SAID THAT!

HA HA!

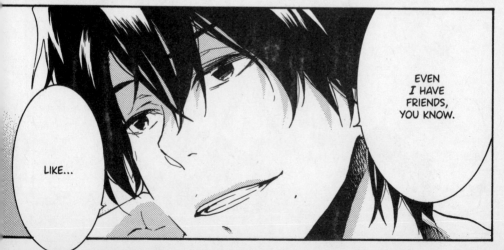

EVEN *I* HAVE FRIENDS, YOU KNOW.

LIKE...

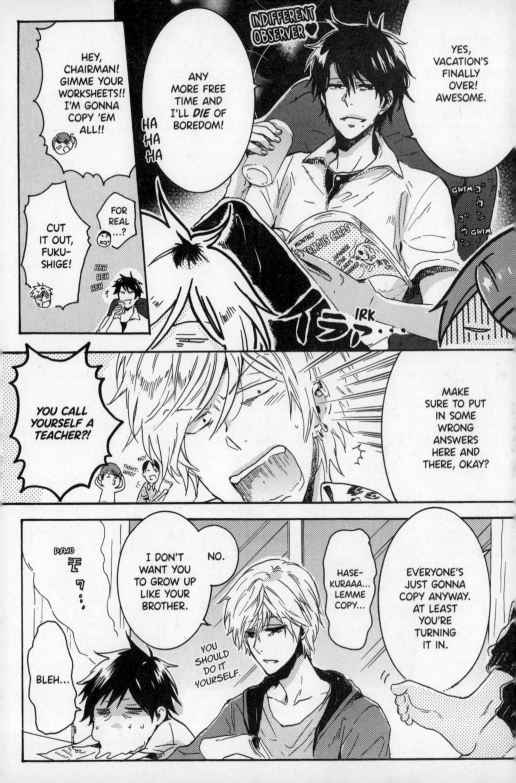

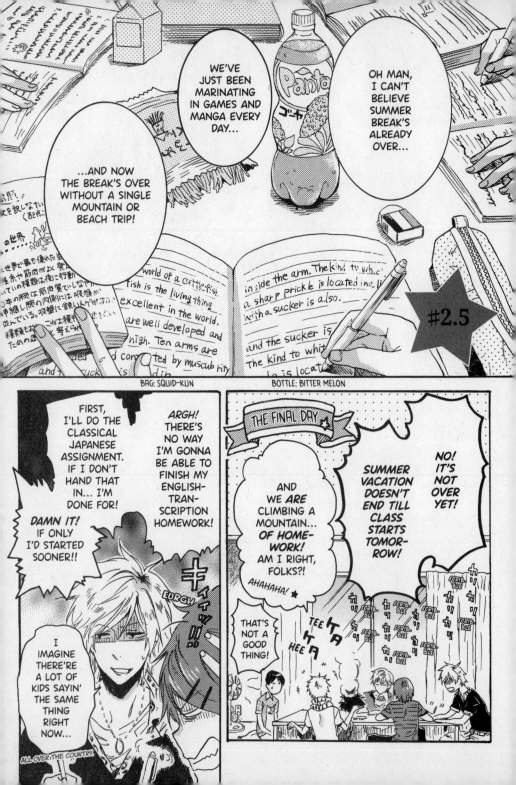

OH MAN, I CAN'T BELIEVE SUMMER BREAK'S ALREADY OVER...

WE'VE JUST BEEN MARINATING IN GAMES AND MANGA EVERY DAY...

...AND NOW THE BREAK'S OVER WITHOUT A SINGLE MOUNTAIN OR BEACH TRIP!

#2.5

BAG: SQUID-KUN

BOTTLE: BITTER MELON

ARGH! THERE'S NO WAY I'M GONNA BE ABLE TO FINISH MY ENGLISH-TRAN-SCRIPTION HOMEWORK!

FIRST, I'LL DO THE CLASSICAL JAPANESE ASSIGNMENT. IF I DON'T HAND THAT IN... I'M DONE FOR!

DAMN IT! IF ONLY I'D STARTED SOONER!!

I IMAGINE THERE'RE A LOT OF KIDS SAYIN' THE SAME THING RIGHT NOW...

ALL OVER THE COUNTRY.

THE FINAL DAY

NO! IT'S NOT OVER YET!

SUMMER VACATION DOESN'T END TILL CLASS STARTS TOMOR-ROW!

AND WE *ARE* CLIMBING A MOUNTAIN... *OF HOME-WORK!* AM I RIGHT, FOLKS?! AHAHAHA!

THAT'S NOT A GOOD THING!

TEE HEE

SCRIB-BLE

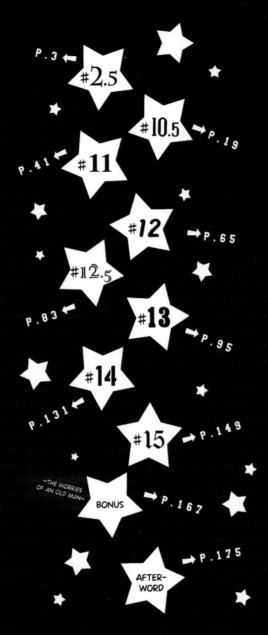

Hitorijime My Hero CONTENTS

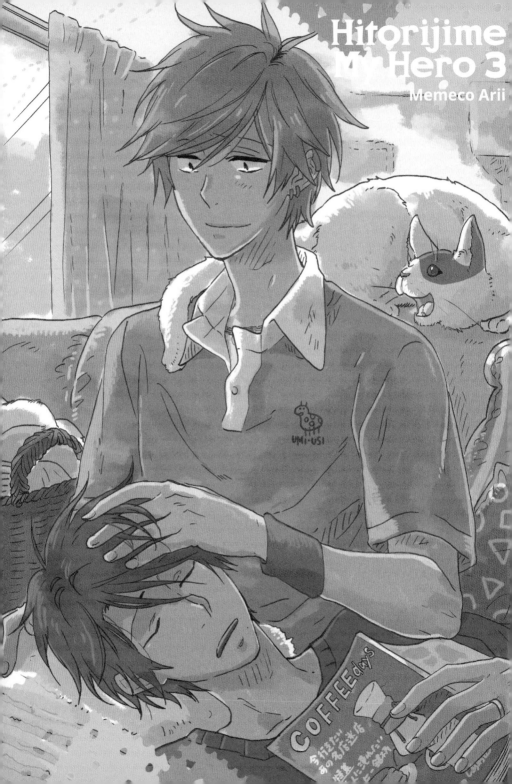